The Myth
of Organizational Culture

The Myth of Organizational Culture

How Leaders Misunderstand the Role of Paradigms and Power

J.W. Traphagan

Jefferson, North Carolina

ISBN (print) 978-1-4766-9699-7
ISBN (ebook) 978-1-4766-5634-2

LIBRARY OF CONGRESS CATALOGING-IN-PUBLICATION DATA

Library of Congress Control Number 2025024949

© 2025 J.W. Traphagan. All rights reserved

No part of this book may be reproduced or transmitted in any form or by any means, electronic or mechanical, including photocopying or recording, or by any information storage and retrieval system, without permission in writing from the publisher.

Front cover image: © VectorMine/ProStockStudio/Shutterstock

Printed in the United States of America

Toplight is an imprint of McFarland & Company, Inc., Publishers

*Box 611, Jefferson, North Carolina 28640
www.toplightbooks.com*

Acknowledgments

This book came about as a result of teaching in the graduate program Human Dimensions of Organizations (HDO) at the University of Texas at Austin. Over the course of about ten years, I taught the core course on qualitative research methods, and for a few years early in the program, I co-taught a course on organizations and culture. I am appreciative of the opportunity to teach in the HDO program and for the insights gained through working with the wonderful colleagues with whom I taught over the years and who challenged me to think in new ways. In particular, I am thankful to Art Markman and Amy Ware, who successively directed the HDO program for most of my time as a faculty member. I was privileged to enjoy many fascinating conversations with my colleagues in HDO, particularly Clay Spinuzzi, with whom I co-taught the course on organizational culture early in the program. His boundless energy and intellectual depth most certainly shaped my ideas about the problems with the organizational culture concept.

I also want to thank the many incredible students I taught throughout my years in the HDO program and then later in the Organizational Dynamics program at the University of Pennsylvania. The list is long and names too numerous to include, so I will simply collectively show my appreciation for these mid-career professionals who changed my outlook both on the business world and on the process of education. Without their ideas, this book could not have been written.

Table of Contents

Acknowledgments   v

Preface   1

Chapter 1. The Problem   5
    Culture Matters   16
    Key Takeaways   19

Chapter 2. What Is Culture?   20
    Defining Culture   22
    Culture Is a Complex Concept   43
    Key Takeaways   49

Chapter 3. Why Organizations Don't Have Cultures   50
    Tacit Value Systems   56
    Key Takeaways   67

Chapter 4. Organizational Ideologies and Paradigms   68
    The Process of Making Our World   76
    Key Takeaways   84

Chapter 5. Power as Productive Force   85
    Power and Organizational Dynamics   99
    Key Takeaways   102

Chapter 6. Promoting Strong Organizations
   by Understanding Productive Power   103
    Productive Power   107
    Key Takeaways   115

Chapter 7. Cultivating an Anthropological Mindset   116
    What Is Research?   128
    The Importance of Power and Self-Awareness   131

Table of Contents

Self-Awareness	137
Key Takeaways	140
Chapter 8. Organizations, Culture, and Change	141
Key Takeaways	154
Works Cited	155
Index	159

Preface

In 2011, I was approached by a psychology professor named Art Markman at the University of Texas at Austin (UT) about my potential interest in joining a new program he was developing. The idea was to create an executive master's degree for mid-career professionals that brought together scholars from disciplines in the social sciences and humanities, rather than the business school, and who had an interest in understanding organizational dynamics as well as in teaching adult learners seeking educational opportunities to enhance their skills and careers. Intrigued, I quickly agreed to join and found myself in the position of being one of the founding faculty in what came to be known as the Program in Human Dimensions of Organizations (HDO). For more than ten years, I taught a course on qualitative research methods for understanding organizations in HDO at UT, and today, I teach a similar course in the Organizational Dynamics graduate program at the University of Pennsylvania. In the early years of HDO, I also team taught a course on organizational culture with Clay Spinuzzi, a professor in the Rhetoric Department at UT. We had a great deal of fun teaching together and I learned much from Clay, as I did from our students. Clay's intellectual enthusiasm and openness to debate is something that I continue to cherish, and our class is among the highlights of my career.

As the HDO program developed, I started leading one-day seminars at UT, and at several outside organizations, that focused on issues in leadership and ethics. These were instrumental in developing my ideas on things like the usefulness of mission and values statements as they relate to the idea of organizational culture. And

Preface

there was a key point that kept bothering me as I taught in the HDO program—the way in which the word "culture" was typically used in conversations and writing about organizations did not reflect much of the recent thinking in anthropology about the culture concept. The more I thought about it, the more I concluded that for the most part the culture concept was employed in fairly unsophisticated ways in the study of organizations and this was hindering our understanding of how organizations work, as well as efforts to address organizational problems and develop good programs intended to promote organizational change. Part of this was a product of a failure among many writing about organizations to carefully define what they mean by culture. But there was also something deeper going on, a problem that had also arisen in anthropology—the word "culture" is quite difficult to define. You may ask here, why is anthropology important in this discussion? The answer is because anthropology is the discipline from which the culture concept emerged as a feature of human social organization to be studied. And anthropologists over the past half-century or so have struggled with how to best define the concept to the point that some have even come to write against using the term at all. In many ways, within anthropology and certainly in the broad public discourse on organizations, the meaning of the word culture has become so diffuse that it's worth questioning its usefulness as an analytical category.

Along with my experiences as a professor in HDO, my research program over the past decade or so has led me to believe many of the themes associated with the organizational culture concept—such as the assumption that culture is about bringing people together and enhancing teamwork—are the product of ethnocentric perspectives, largely American, that shape quite a bit of writing on organizational dynamics. In the second decade of the 21st century, I embarked on an ethnographic research project focused on understanding the lives and ideas of entrepreneurs and small business owners in rural Japan. The product of that research was a book called *Cosmopolitan Rurality, Depopulation, and Entrepreneurial Ecosystems in 21st-Century*

Preface

Japan (Cambria Press, 2020). One of the many things I learned through that project was the fact that entrepreneurs and small business owners in places like rural Japan don't necessarily think about their goals, businesses, or even what it means to be an entrepreneur, in ways that parallel what is often written about entrepreneurialism and small-business ownership in American books and articles on the subject. This pushed me to think about a key point of this book—that organizations don't have cultures, but are, instead, embedded in cultural contexts that profoundly shape how people within those organizations think and behave. It was that line of inquiry that led me down an intellectual path along which I eventually trundled off an abyss where the very idea of organizational culture became problematic in my head. This book is my attempt to address this issue and to work through the problems of how we can theorize about and understand how organizations operate without resorting to vague, often intellectually unsophisticated, appeals to the organizational culture concept.

My sincere hope is that readers will find the pages that follow thought-provoking, even if, in the end, they disagree with or even hate (as some have) the ideas I present. The goal of social science, and in my view of any intellectual endeavor, is not to find *the* answers to our problems, but to contribute to an ongoing discourse in which we keep thinking about how to conceptualize human social behavior and organizational patterns. We get some answers as we engage in this discourse, but those answers are always contingent, because the contexts in which individuals and organizations operate are constantly evolving. There are no definitive answers to our question, only tentative ones. And the purpose of intellectual discourse is to raise ideas, throw them out into the world, and have other people chew on those ideas while accepting the possibility that all or part of what got thrown into the public eye may be misguided, in need of further elaboration, or simply wrong. I'm okay with being wrong, even if my goal is to get it right. Good science and good research, in general, is open to the possibility of getting it wrong. We learn

Preface

as much, or more, from our missteps as we do from our successes. Unfortunately, this is not a concept well understood in modern society (at least in the U.S.) and it contributes to a broad social atmosphere in which people misunderstand how science works and desire *the* correct answers to their questions, rather than an environment in which the discourse and the process of questioning is what matters most as a means to grow in our thinking and understanding of the world. Good critical thinking is about the process, not the answers. Of course, I think I got it right in the pages that follow, but it is up to the reader to decide if that's the case. I hope this book will stimulate people interested in understanding how organizations work to think deeply about usefulness of the organizational culture concept, even if, in the end, they conclude I got it all wrong.

CHAPTER 1

The Problem

When I was in college in the early 1980s, I spent my summers working as a temporary employee, known as a TAG, for a computer company known as Digital Equipment Corporation (DEC). I did data entry, scheduled meetings and air travel for managers, and answered a lot of phone calls. Jobs at DEC were coveted by people living in Massachusetts, because the company was known as being good to its employees, with excellent benefits, and was growing rapidly with the ever-expanding computer industry. My mother worked there as a paralegal, so I knew quite a bit about the DEC "culture," from the good pay to the annual gift of a turkey for every U.S. employee at Thanksgiving. Started in the late 1950s by two researchers at MIT, Ken Olsen and Harlan Anderson, with $70,000 in venture capital and Ken's garage, DEC by the mid-1980s was the second largest computer company in the world, placed only behind IBM. The company had 130,000 employees and $14 billion in worldwide sales at its peak. It was a leader in networked computers and in 1977 introduced the VAX 11/780, the world's first 1MIPS machine. Designed to compete with IBM mainframes, VAX computers could be connected to create powerful VAXclusters and DEC's products were found in government offices, universities, and many businesses.

Working at DEC was fun. There was an atmosphere that seemed relaxed and anti-hierarchical, in contrast to the image of IBM as staid and proper. I was once told by a boss of mine at a software company I worked for a few years later a story about what it was like working at IBM at the time. He said that he came to the office one day with a tie that was too bright a color of red, so his boss pulled out a pair of scissors and cut it off, telling him to go home and put on a proper tie. That wouldn't have happened at DEC. Software engineers and many others didn't even wear ties, and the "business casual" in some offices was a T-shirt and shorts. There were employee appreciation days as well as an excellent pension program, and the company paid tuition for higher degrees like an MBA. And Ken Olsen, who never took the title CEO, was just known as Ken around the company, including when you happened to see him in the hallway. "Hi, Ken," was often heard around the halls of The Mill, the headquarters for the company that was a renovated textile mill in Maynard, Massachusetts.

Much was written about Ken and he even appeared on the cover of *Forbes* as America's most successful entrepreneur. One writer said of Ken's style:

> Olsen himself, through his informal behavior, implied that he did not take his position of power all that seriously. Group members argued as much with him as with each other and even interrupted him from time to time. His status did show up, however, in the occasional lectures he delivered to the group when he felt that members did not understand something or were "wrong" about something. At such times, Olsen could become very emotionally excited in a way that other members of the group never did [Schein, 2010].

Humble in his self-presentation, Ken had a modest office in the Mill, drove a Ford Pinto to the office for a long time, and refused to have a reserved parking space. These behaviors endeared him to employees, who spoke highly of him even if they had never met him. He was credited with creating a "culture of innovation" that empowered employees and was characterized by expressly stated values such as "Do the right thing," an oft-cited maxim around the company. As you walked around any of the main DEC facilities, it was hard not to see the open-office architecture, informality of dress, and regular interaction among employees as they discussed projects. DEC was sometimes described as having an academic culture, with an emphasis on critique and debate. The company pursued linkages with universities that were strong in engineering, like Carnegie Mellon University

Chapter 1. The Problem

in Pittsburgh, and encouraged cross-fertilization with the academic world.

Ken's goal was to have absolute integrity in designing, manufacturing, and selling. He saw his company as highly ethical, and emphasized the values associated with the Protestant work ethic—honesty, hard work, high standards of personal morality, professionalism, personal responsibility, and integrity. When I started at DEC in the mid–1980s, everything looked like the company would be around for a long time. It was hitting on all cylinders, most employees liked working there, and leadership was admired and respected.

Only a few years later, in the 1990s, DEC abruptly collapsed. Decision-makers had failed to read changes in the computer industry arising with the arrival of microcomputers like the IBM PC and Apple II, intended for personal use. Ken was notoriously cited in many media and other publications as saying back in 1977 that "there is no reason for any individual to have a computer in his home." As personal computers became a desired product for home use, DEC quickly shifted from being viewed as innovative to being out-of-step with the times (Centre for Computing History, n.d.).

As DEC grew in the 1980s, it became increasingly hierarchical. There was more bureaucracy and many in the company complained about a loss of creativity and innovation. It seemed that the attitude had shifted from thinking about the best engineered product selling itself to "think customer," which was a huge sign at the top of the entrance stairs in the building where I worked in 1988. DEC had become a vast multi-national corporation with offices around the world. I actually met my wife while working at DEC in Massachusetts—she was working in the Tokyo office. And while DEC struggled to compete with California start-ups like Sun Microsystems, the sales force grew and the number of suits and walled offices expanded. DEC was big, it was still generally viewed as a very good work environment, and it was in trouble.

In 1992, Ken was replaced by Bob Palmer as president of the company. Palmer was also granted the title of CEO. DEC underwent

The Myth of Organizational Culture

a restructuring process and in Q3 of that year lost $260.5 million. There was some improvement in 1993, but in 1994, DEC reported a $183 million loss. Its stock, which had once been close to $200 a share, had dropped to $23 and the workforce was down to 92,000. Palmer began to sell off parts of DEC to keep the company afloat, and in 1998 what remained of the company was sold to Compaq. At the time of the sale DEC had shrunk to less than half of its former size to only 53,000 employees. By 2002, Compaq had merged with HP and virtually all signs of DEC and its "culture" had disappeared—less than twenty years after the company was peaking in the 1980s it was gone.

In fact, the only sign of DEC that remains in Massachusetts today, after so many years during which it was the dominant employer in the state, is the Digital Credit Union (DCU). DCU was the credit union owned by the company and used by many of its employees, it survived as a separate business after DEC was purchased by Compaq. I suspect many in Massachusetts who use DCU today have no idea about its history with DEC, an observation confirmed when I asked my students at Clark University, in Worcester, Massachusetts, where an indoor arena known as the DCU Center is located, if they knew about DEC or about the history of DCU. Unsurprisingly, none of them had any idea.

What happened? Was the problem DEC's corporate culture? Company leadership certainly did present a set of values in their behaviors, largely associated with Ken's take on the Protestant Work Ethic—frugality, hard work, limited hierarchy, etc.—although these were certainly not uncontested, particularly as the company grew. People talked about a DEC culture and the company was even written about in books on business due to its perceived positive working environment (Peters & Waterman, Jr., 1984). It's important to recognize that the "culture" at DEC, if there was one, reflected the individual values of its leader—Ken Olsen. And despite the fact that those values seemed good—absolute integrity, honesty, hard work—the company failed. One is left wondering why this happened. Was

Chapter 1. The Problem

leadership incompetent? Was there something wrong with those values, that Ken so cherished, in a business environment? Was the organizational culture actually screwed up in some way?

The answers to these questions are important, but also rather complex. That said, one point that I want to emphasize here is that the problem wasn't with DEC's *culture*. The company was run by engineers with the idea that good products would sell themselves. DEC made great products, treated its employees well, and had what might be viewed as a good (at least for Americans) corporate environment that encouraged debate, discussion, egalitarianism, and supported employee development. What could go wrong? It certainly seems as though DEC had a good organizational culture, at least if we define organizational culture in the way that is typical in studies of organizational dynamics or on the vast sea of blogs about organizational culture on the Internet.

In reality, it's important to recognize that DEC had no culture of its own. Instead, it was *embedded* in a larger cultural flow that included technological innovations which didn't seem to fit well with DEC's business model. Those technological innovations were changing the way people thought about and used computers. In the end, DEC crashed because its leadership was out of step with the culture in which the company was embedded. Its problems were not its own culture or values, but the inability of leaders to see that it was *part of a culture and that the larger culture it inhabited was changing rapidly*. This is a subtle, but important, point that shapes my argument throughout this book. The idea of organizational culture tends to downplay and even ignore the influence of the cultural context within which any organization is immersed. Organizations are not stand-alone structures with their own cultures; they are intertwined with the economic, political, social, and cultural contexts within which they operate.

Why didn't DEC's leadership see that changing environment before it was too late? If DEC had a culture of innovation, how could it have so thoroughly failed to innovate? If the company had good

The Myth of Organizational Culture

values—integrity, hard work, openness to critique, and honesty certainly seem like good values to me—then why didn't those values carry the organization through difficult times? The answer has to do with DEC's engineering centered paradigm and the ideology that shaped its paradigm. I'll talk about paradigms more later in the book, but for now I want to spend a few moments explaining why I use the word paradigm instead of culture. Back in the early 1960s a philosopher of science named Thomas Kuhn wrote a revolutionary book—it had a good title for a revolutionary book, because it's called *The Structure of Scientific Revolutions*. Kuhn changed the way many scholars understood the process of scientific discovery and he coined a new use for the word *paradigm*, defining it as "the practices that define a scientific discipline at certain point in time" (Kuhn & Hacking, 2012). Kuhn limits his definition to the scientific community and presents a scientific paradigm as, "universally recognized scientific achievements that, for a time, provide model problems and solutions to a community of practitioners" (Kuhn, 1996, 10). What this means is that a paradigm sets the parameters for what can be observed and queried, the types of questions that are acceptable to ask, the ways in which those questions are structured, and the methods by which scientific investigations should be pursued and results interpreted. Kuhn argues that scientists generally operate within the framework of "normal science," where the prevailing model for inquiry dominates the ways in which research is conducted and shapes cognition, or thinking, itself for most people within the scientific community. However, these periods of relative stability are punctuated by occasional periods where the model undergoes a rapid and significant change, usually as a result of a new perspective that emerges and shakes up how scientists see the world itself. Einstein's theory of relativity is an example of the type of worldview-breaking theory that undermined the prevailing paradigm and generated new ideas and experiments that eventually produced a new paradigm for scientific inquiry into the nature of physical reality. It should not be assumed that all scientists interpret the prevailing paradigm in the

Chapter 1. The Problem

same way; in fact, it's because some scientists challenge a given paradigm that moments of crisis arise and scientists are forced to rethink their ideas about the world. Challenges to a prevailing paradigm are at the root of innovation.

Kuhn's notion has similarities to the often-used definition of organizational culture as "the way we do things around here," but there are some important differences. For one thing, paradigms are culturally based, not cultures by themselves. If you talk to two different medical specialists, one who practices Western biomedicine and another who practices Chinese medicine, you will find that they may have different assumptions about the causes of and best ways to treat disease. There often are overlaps, but the differences are real and the ways they do things reflect different values and ideas about health, illness, and the nature of being human. The two approaches inhabit different medical paradigms that are profoundly shaped by the larger cultural contexts in which those paradigms live and operate. At the core, these differences are related to how the relationship between nature and humans is understood. In the Chinese philosophical framework, there is an emphasis on balance and a sense that humans are one element of the natural world. In the Western model, there is a history of separating humans and nature and a tendency to view nature as something that can be manipulated or even conquered (Blackbourn, 2007). Interestingly, this perspective on the natural world is quite similar to how many in fields such as organizational dynamics understand culture—as something that can be manipulated and shaped fairly precisely. As we will see, this underestimates the complexity of behavior in groups (Graziano, 2023).

Paradigms do a variety of things to influence decision-making. In the sciences, they limit what we decide to study and research. They shape the types of questions we ask. And they influence how results are interpreted. In many ways, a paradigm is like a dogma, a term people use to refer to things they think are true or seem good without spending much time questioning their validity. In the sciences,

The Myth of Organizational Culture

unlike many religious frameworks, however, skepticism is built-in to the dogma, which tends to promote eventual questioning of accepted modes of thought and explanation. Kuhn thought that paradigms could absorb a degree of error, but as a paradigm matured it would encounter so much error that there would be a shift or a revolutionary change in the entire way the scientific discipline sees the world. This is what happened when Einstein's ideas about relativity dramatically changed the scope of Newton's laws and ultimately changed how we see the universe. And the outcome of this type of shift is what Kuhn described as a scientific revolution in which a disruptive scientific idea displaces the existing paradigm and a new paradigm eventually emerges, generating a return to normal science, even if what is normal has itself changed significantly. The key point I want readers to take away form Kuhn's notion is not simply that a paradigm is a way of looking at the world—it shapes, deeply, how scientists think about and interpret what they observe. In other words, the paradigm operating at a given time shapes the cognitive modeling in the brain that scientists use to observe and interpret physical reality (Margenau, *The Nature of Physical Reality*, 1950). It shapes the way they construct their understanding of reality itself.

For the purposes of this book, I want to define what I mean by the term paradigm as it relates to organizational dynamics very clearly. While I will borrow from Kuhn's notion of the scientific paradigm, I want to limit my definition to what I will refer to as an *organizational paradigm*. An organizational paradigm *is a broadly recognized framework used for identifying what constitutes achievement or success and determining what are accepted and acceptable modes of practice for members of an organization or institution. It shapes the ways in which problems are identified and solved, who is responsible for determining how problems should be identified and solved, and setting the parameters that limit the types of questions that can be asked, the ways in which ideas can be challenged, and how the larger world or reality in which the organization operates should be interpreted.* In ways similar to what Kuhn describes for the

Chapter 1. The Problem

scientific world, organizational paradigms can enter periods of crisis, in which basic accepted modes of practice and values are challenged and reformed or discarded. Note that my definition does not include mission statements nor bulleted lists of organizational values. While these can play a role in articulating what is viewed—usually by leaders—as important components of an organizational paradigm, they are actually only a very small part of what's going on. I will return to this later in the book.

Paradigms are shaped by ideologies, which are often implicit. There are many ways to define the term ideology and we can think about various type of ideologies, such as political, economic, or religious ideologies. For my purposes here, I define an ideology as *a largely coherent system of ideas and beliefs that rely on a set of basic assumptions people use to give those ideas legitimacy*. There is usually a normative—meaning moral—aspect to how the ideology functions and there is always an internal logic or structure within which ideas are formed, interpreted, and expressed. Ideologies can be understood as ideational frameworks through which humans experience, process, and express meanings and values within the context of social life (Eagleton, *Ideology: An Introduction*, 1991). Ideologies naturalize and often universalize beliefs and ideas in such a way that they seem self-evident and thus need not be critiqued nor contested. This is one of the reasons ideologies are so important in creating a sense of identity for particular groups—they usually exclude rival ideas and perspectives, a behavior which, in turn, legitimizes the ideas of those who adhere to a particular ideology.

Going back to DEC, the building I worked in also housed the marketing arm of DEC and I occasionally heard marketing folks coming out of meetings complaining about the inability of the engineers who led the company to show much interest in the marketing and selling side of the business. We can view this as the pressure point where the problem arose for the organization. There were competing paradigms operating simultaneously within the company. One favored an engineering-based model of operation, while the

The Myth of Organizational Culture

other favored a marketing-based model. And the engineering paradigm was dominant, most likely due to the engineering background and personal influence of Ken and other high level leadership as well as the fact that it had been highly successful in driving organizational growth—until it wasn't. Until the late 1980s, the engineering paradigm had worked quite well. DEC easily sold its products and the company grew rapidly. But new innovations arose, like the PC and laptop, that challenged the usefulness of DEC's products and also changed the context of computer use more broadly in society. In essence, DEC had entered into an environment that represented a crisis for its organizational paradigm, not unlike the type of Kuhn describes arising occasionally in the scientific community.

Regular people could buy computers and use them at home, but DEC's VAX computers weren't designed for that—and the high-end versions of those smaller computers were becoming competitive with DEC's products in terms of things like millions of instructions per second (MIPS). I remember when I worked as a TAG listening to conversations among my boss and other managers about why MIPS really wasn't that important as a measure of the quality of a computer. The paradigm under which DEC operated tended to blind corporate leaders to changes happening elsewhere in the computer industry and often directed the thinking of leaders away from concepts that were coming to dominate how "good" was defined in relation to use and performance of computer architecture. They missed the boat on the PC and on the emergence of laptops, which led to a crisis for the company as profits dropped and its products no longer seemed to clearly fit the reality—the worldview about computer use—in which they were being sold. DEC struggled to compete with companies like Sun Microsystems, with their compact workstations, which were taking away customers by providing faster computers for less money and assuring potential users that they could connect their products to other brands (Richards, 1989). Reality, of course, is ever-changing, particularly when it comes to human social organization. And this is what DEC struggled to respond to as the market

Chapter 1. The Problem

and the nature of computer use changed rapidly throughout the social and business context in which the company was embedded. Put another way, the organizational paradigm at DEC failed to reflect and respond to changing technological, business, and social contexts and when this happens an organization is likely to enter into a period of crisis.

Of course, leadership at DEC didn't just sit around and wring their hands. They assessed the situation and responded to the changing context with new products. In the mid–1990s DEC built some very good laptops in their HighNote line that received strong reviews. The company also developed new chip technologies, particularly their 64-bit Alpha processor, that powered an array of new products, but also became the center of a major patent infringement lawsuit that DEC filed against Intel which filed a counter-suit against DEC for violating property rights (Levine, 1997). The conflict led to the sale of DEC's semiconductor manufacturing operations to Intel in a huge settlement in which DEC would continue to develop chip technologies, but within Intel's newly acquired facilities.

As DEC responded to the changing environment it got better at marketing and made commercials touting the bright screens and sleek designs of their laptops. There was an effort to continue developing its excellent technologies while also responding to a market in which computers were becoming increasingly used by a wide variety of people and organizations. Clearly, by the mid–1990s the company had undergone a paradigm shift and was emerging from crisis, but it was too late. The cultural context in which DEC was embedded changed faster than the company's leaders could react, in part because engineers had so profoundly shaped the paradigm under which DEC grew, an organizational paradigm that did not respond easily to a cultural context in which marketing was becoming more important than engineering in many ways. Companies like Apple were producing relatively inexpensive computers that were easy to use and looked cool, and that attracted non-techie customers more than what was under the hood. In the end, DEC collapsed

The Myth of Organizational Culture

not because its products were poor, but because the organizational paradigm it had operated and grown with no longer fit with the larger social context in which the company needed to operate. This is important: DEC died not so much because of failed products, but because of failed understanding of its social and cultural context, which itself was a product of its organizational paradigm. I emphasize social over business here, because there is much more to DEC's collapse than a poor business model. Leaders at DEC simply were unable to grasp, until it was too late, that the organization was embedded in a much larger social context and that social context was not well-aligned with the organizational paradigm DEC had developed over several successful decades designing, manufacturing, and selling its computers.

CULTURE MATTERS

Culture matters when we think about organizations like companies, educational institutions, medical institutions, or government institutions. And it contributes to their successes and failures. But it's not a *property* of those organizations. This is where many in fields like organizational dynamics have missed the boat. Culture is typically presented as an attribute or feature of an organization that can be managed and controlled with the right leadership skills. It would be nice if it were that simple; however, culture is quite a bit more complex than this perspective would lead us to believe. And, as noted above, one of the key problems with the organizational culture idea is that it tends to ignore the fact that organizations, themselves, are embedded in larger cultural contexts that significantly shape how those organizations operate. Organizations have paradigms that shape the ways things get done and the decisions that are made. But those paradigms are usually not so much about culture as they are about power relationships that influence how people work and what they think is normal. When the cultural context

Chapter 1. The Problem

an organization lives in changes, but ideas about what's normal inside the organization don't change, the organization is in trouble (Alvesson & Sveningsson, 2024). *In the end, that's what killed DEC.*

DEC, of course, is only one example. Many people in the U.S. are aware of the disastrous case of Enron. After California's failed experiment with water deregulation in the 1990s, Enron's leaders decided to build on its already international presence in energy and expand into the water industry. It made big deals in the UK and Argentina and by 2000 the company's reputation was riding high and CEO Ken Lay and McKinsey consultant Jeff Skilling were viewed as visionary strategists and top business leaders. Unfortunately, Enron's rapid expansion outran its ability to fund itself, so leaders secretly created a complex web of financing vehicles that were secured against Enron's rapidly rising share price. Enron failed to generate sufficient cash flow, while spending huge amounts on expansion. The entire scheme imploded in scandal.

Some analysists attributed an important part of Enron's problems to its intense culture of performance, buttressed by incentive schemes that both promised and delivered large financial awards for high performers. When combined with a strategy in which aggressive accounting practices and the use of market valuations were used to produce artificially large earnings to hide poor profitability, the company's collapse was inevitable. At the beginning of December 2001, Enron filed for the biggest bankruptcy the United States had yet seen.

But the problem here wasn't that Enron had a bad culture. It had a model built within a context of economic growth, a rapidly rising stock market, low unemployment, and a general optimism that began with the fall of the Soviet Union and reflected things like rapidly dropping crime rates in the U.S. Neoliberal policies aimed at generating economic growth through deregulation and privatization had generated an American business climate viewed as vibrant, healthy, and in which the sky was the limit when it came to making

The Myth of Organizational Culture

money. Indeed, the government was helping it all along when bipartisan majorities signed the Financial Services Modernization Act of 1999 that collapsed firewalls between investment banks and commercial banks. The competition driven neoliberal lifestyle was so good that even coffee got much better with the expansion of Starbucks. Enron's problem was in part due to the greed of leadership, but that greed combined with unbridled optimism about making money had developed into a paradigm for operation that reflected broader values of un-checked growth, unregulated corporations, and general optimism that permeated 1990s American culture. When combined with personal greed among Enron's leaders, it became a dangerous and disastrous cocktail.

People often mistake organizational paradigms for organizational cultures. My aim in this book is to explore how and why this happens and explain why missing this point is a problem for organizations and can even lead an organization to fail. To state it briefly: Organizations don't fail because a culture is bad, but because leadership often doesn't clearly see when an organization's way of doing things is poorly aligned to the larger cultural context. Individuals *and* organizations are *parts* of cultures that shape how they make decisions and how those decisions influence the success of any group. And those cultures are always changing. Organizations don't really have cultures. They do have ways of doing things and these ways are better thought of as paradigms, with complex power relationships among employees and other stakeholders that influence what can and cannot be done. When leaders lack cognizance of how their organizational paradigm is connected and exists in relation to the cultural context in which that organization functions, there is a good chance problems are going to arise.

Following the Enron disaster, and many others, organizational leaders have become increasingly interested in the idea of organizational culture. There are numerous websites on organizational culture and interest in organizational culture has spread to other countries. I was called by a writer for London's *Raconteur* recently,

Chapter 1. The Problem

who explained he wanted to interview me because there is a growing interest in organizational culture in the UK. The article he wrote notes that culture is a "soft concept" that's hard to define and goes on to emphasize how important culture is to creating a profitable organization. An EU website devoted to organizational culture lets readers know that "the most important thing about culture is that it's the only sustainable point of difference for any organization. Anyone can copy a company's strategy, but nobody can copy their culture" (Carayol, 2012). The website goes on to explain that culture is an organization's "immune system" protecting it from disaster.

None of these dramatic claims about culture are really explained, and as will become clear in the chapters that follow, I think most of them are wrong. But they point to the fact that organizational culture is a hot topic—even if it's not usually very well defined. In the next chapter, I will focus on defining culture and showing the significant problems anthropologists—who first used the term as a way of understanding human groups back in the 19th century—when they try to define and make use of the term.

Key Takeaways

- *Organizations do not have cultures; they are embedded within cultural contexts that shape how those organizations operate.*
- *Organizational leaders run into problems when they fail to understand and accurately assess the cultural context in which their organization is operating.*
- *Organizations have paradigms, with ideologies and complex power relationships among stakeholders, that shape both individual and collective behavior in relation to larger social and cultural contexts.*

CHAPTER 2

What Is Culture?

A few years ago, I wrote an article for the *Harvard Business Review* (HBR) asking if "company culture" was a meaningful idea (Traphagan, 2015). My answer was, and still is, "no." I argued that the culture concept leads us to gloss over the complex realities of organizational environments and can lead organizational decision-makers to misunderstand the causes of success and failure. It's much easier to ascribe success or failure to an abstract concept like culture than it is to specific features of organizational structure and practice, such as power relationships, that may influence behavior. Reliance on the culture concept also downplays the fact that change is not simply a product of conscious decision-making, but a constant of any social context that can only be controlled in limited ways through attempts at social engineering an organization through activities like culture change programs.

There were a few interesting responses to my HBR article. Some people talked about it in their blogs on organizational culture. Hilton Barbour wrote a nice piece for Global Brand Leaders in which he explained and expanded on some of what I wrote in that HBR article (Barbour, 2015). Although Barbour sees a need to retain the organizational culture idea, he drastically limits its value to only those situations when you're "obsessing about how your Culture can become an accelerant for your Strategy." It's an interesting point, because it conceptualizes culture as a specific component that contributes to execution of a business strategy. I'm not sure I agree with this, but Barbour's ideas are important because they give a specific way to think about the usefulness of the culture concept and define that

Chapter 2. What Is Culture?

concept in a much less vague way than the usual, "the way we do things around here" approach.

The most enjoyable response was a piece in *Forbes* by Don Pontefract, who had a melodramatic reaction to his morning cereal after reading my words (he wrote that he nearly "choked to death" on his cereal ... or maybe it was my writing?) (Pontefract, 2015). Pontefract believes organizations don't need to give up the company culture idea, but should just work with employees to "craft common operating principles (behaviors, tools, processes and so on) that connects [sic] the entire organization as one." In other words, they should use the corporate culture idea as a tool for social engineering aimed at creating unified attitudes and ideas about the organization and its goals. This sounds a lot more like totalitarianism than it does culture to me—it's a political maneuver grounded in an authoritarian mindset that assumes social engineering can address organizational dynamics by generating a common ideological framework. You don't need to read the rest of this book to understand that I think this is a ridiculous idea and a remarkably poor understanding of culture.

It would be nice for leaders (particularly those with authoritarian inclinations) if culture were a simple tool people could use to engineer common values and ideas. But that's not what culture is about, nor is the social engineering approach a useful way to think about organizations. Why? Because culture isn't only about unity; it's also about division. In this chapter, my aim is to consider how to define the culture concept and give some thought to how that concept is used in organizational dynamics studies as well as anthropology. Part of my purpose in discussing these ideas is to show that the typical definition of culture used in the discussion of organizations is facile. The idea that an organizational culture is "the way we do things around here" is not helpful, because it ignores a matrix of variables that contribute to how things get done—such as power distribution, individual and group identity, local ideological themes, and the larger cultural environment in which any organization is

The Myth of Organizational Culture

embedded. Another problem is that culture doesn't just involve common values and ways of doing things; it also involves ways in which we contest and contradict common values and ways of doing things.

Defining Culture

In his *Forbes* piece Pontefract quotes Greg Smith, who wrote an editorial to the *New York Times* ("Why I Am Leaving Goldman Sachs," March 14, 2012) in which he claims that culture was a vital part of the success of Goldman Sachs (GS) when he worked there. It was the "secret sauce that made the place great and allowed us to earn our clients' trust for 143 years." Smith states in his *Times* piece that the collapse of that culture is why he decided to leave, and Pontefract sings Smith's praises, stating that he successfully depicts what "true" company culture should be about—"concepts such as teamwork, integrity, humility, and finding the processes, behaviours, and mechanisms inside the company to put your 'customers first.'" That, for Pontefract, is "indeed what true 'company culture' is all about." It's a good idea to be skeptical when someone talks about the one "true" way of doing things, and Pontefract's representation of culture through Smith's GS experience is a good example.

Many problems can be found in this definition, not the least of which is the fact that Smith seems to believe that somehow the culture of GS remained constant over the course of nearly a century and a half. Think about that for a minute—he appears to believe that GS got through two world wars, a global depression, and the Cold War, without changing its culture. That's impressive. It's also impossible. No organization could function successfully in a constantly changing social, economic, and political environment without itself changing. Smith's secret sauce lacks piquancy.

Thinking even slightly about what Smith is claiming underscores how simplistic a perspective on culture is being presented by Smith and his fan Pontefract. And it's this naive viewpoint Pontefract uses

Chapter 2. What Is Culture?

to conceptualize culture in terms of tidy and unambiguous features assumed to be intrinsic to the culture concept and universally applicable to human behavior. In other words, Pontefract is stating that there is only one possible definition for organizational culture which casts organizational culture entirely independent of larger political, economic, historical, and social forces in which any company is embedded. And he knows what it is! Culture, for Pontefract, is all about teamwork and getting along together. This is a rather narrow perspective that presents culture as a thing, rather than a process (more on this later) and also is far too simplistic to be of much use in understanding how organizations operate. It also assumes beliefs like putting one's customer first or emphasizing teamwork are the only possible way to think about a business. This isn't true. We are, in fact, seeing changing ideas about the priorities in business practices where there is growing interest in putting the employee first which, it is believed, will lead to happy workers who do well by customer (Rasmus Hougaard, "The Power of Putting People First," *Forbes*). If we focus on teamwork, what exactly is meant by that? Teamwork refers to group involvement that contributes to the efficiency of the whole, but the way this happens can vary considerably depending on context and values. Even within a particular organization, like a university, the nature of teamwork can vary—it is different in the classroom for me, where teamwork isn't necessarily all that important if I'm lecturing, as opposed to working on a committee. Another problem is that people don't just blithely become part of a team, they interpret the group and think about what it means to be a member of the team and, thus, what teamwork means in that context. The point that's important here is that there is not a single correct way—contrary to Pontefract's claims—to build something we might call an organizational culture if we must use that term. And regardless of whatever we might build, any organizational culture is part of a larger cultural context in which concepts like teamwork take on complex meanings or may not be particularly meaningful at all.

In his book, *Culture Is the Way*, Matt Mayberry devotes quite a bit of electronic ink to the question "What is culture?" and I think he certainly does better than Pontefract in thinking about the problem. But, then, I also think the bar is pretty low when it comes to Pontefract's ideas. As Mayberry notes, it's not easy to answer this question. He opens the second chapter, titled with the same question, by quoting business theorist and psychologist Edgar Schein that culture "is the deeper level of basic assumptions and beliefs that are shared by members of an organization, that operate unconsciously and define the basic 'taken for granted' fashion of an organization's view of itself and its environment." He then goes on to work the definition of culture in some detail. He comes up with some pithy catchphrases to encapsulate culture: it's the "lifeblood of organizational excellence. The core. The energy, The genetic code...." It's the "X-factor," he states quoting Noah Rabinowitz, senior partner and global head of Hay Group's Leadership Development Practice. "It's the invisible glue that holds an organization together and ultimately makes the difference between whether an organization is able to succeed in the market or not." In short, Mayberry believes that culture is about how well any organization does what it does, particularly "behind closed doors." Culture is about "collective mindsets," "consistent results," and "repeated efforts and actions" (Mayberry, 2023). Later in the chapter, Mayberry describes a conversation he had in which he defines culture as "everything and it's nearly impossible to place too much of an emphasis on it ... you must identify your culture targets and then define what your culture stands for" (Mayberry, 2023).

If you think about it, the "culture is everything" definition is analytically useless. Because it is so nebulous, it does little work in terms of helping us to understand organizational dynamics. One way to understand this problem is to do a little thought experiment. Take a moment to define "the sky." What did you come up with? Did you define it as blue? Did you define it as everything above you? If you think even a little into the problem, it becomes quite difficult to define the sky. It's blue, except when it isn't, such as at night or when it's cloudy. It's everything above you, but that's a meaningless

Chapter 2. What Is Culture?

definition because it essentially means the sky is the entire universe. We can come up with better definitions, such as the region of the upper atmosphere or outer space visible from the surface of the Earth. If we keep thinking, it will be possible to further refine that definition.

Precision in defining concepts matters. It helps us to create clear frameworks for analysis, which are necessary if the concepts we use are going to be analytically productive. This is not to say that we can't learn anything from vague definitions. Indeed, the hazy definitions of culture Mayberry and many others employ in studies of organizational dynamics capture just how difficult a variable culture is to discuss, particularly with any conceptual sophistication. It will be useful to devote a few pages to how anthropologists have imagined the notion of culture. It's also important to recognize that, despite being the core concept of anthropology, scientists working in this field have never really been able to come to a firm agreement on what it is that they are studying.

The term was first used in academic writing by British anthropologist Edward B. Tylor in his 1871 book, *Primitive Culture*, to describe learned behavior in humans. Tylor argued that culture is "that complex whole which includes knowledge, belief, art, law, morals, custom, and any other capabilities and habits acquired by man as a member of society" (Tylor, 1871). Sounds a lot like Mayberry's approach. It's what I refer to as a kitchen sink definition, which is usually not particularly useful from an analytical perspective, because it's so broad that we can't leave anything out—culture is everything that people do as members of society. Despite its problems, this definition raises two important points that became cornerstones of anthropological thinking about culture: (1) culture is acquired, meaning that it is learned, and (2) whatever it is, culture involves collections of people—it isn't solitary.

One problem with culture that Tylor's definition manages to capture, and is also evident in Mayberry's ideas, is that whatever culture is, it's hard to isolate, which also means it's quite difficult to analyze systematically. Culture so thoroughly permeates what humans do, and what seems to differentiate humans from other animals, that it is virtually impossible to determine where its boundaries lie in relation to human behavior. How do we identify which things that humans do are produced by culture and which things are not? Crying, for example, is a biologically driven behavior. Humans cry from birth. However, humans do not all cry in the same way. If you observe crying behavior in different cultures, you will notice that there are variations in how and why people cry. In some social contexts people may wail, in others not so much. In some social contexts, men may be expected to suppress tears, while in others it may be allowed or expected that men cry. There is a great deal of literature in anthropology on how the human body is shaped by culture. Basic biological functions, like walking, are also profoundly shaped by cultural context. We pick up how we move our bodies by watching others in much the same way we pick up our native languages (Bourdieu, 1977).

Another example will be instructive. If you are a religious person, you probably believe in the existence of some type of deity. Why? Is it because that deity is real and you've observed it in action? If it is, then why are there so many deities that humans believe exist? Why do some people believe in multiple deities while others think there's only one? Why do some religions, like Christianity, have a creator deity while others, like Buddhism, don't? Think hard about this next question: If you believe your religion is true, what do you base that belief on? Is it because you have empirical evidence for its verity? Or is it because someone else told you it's true, perhaps when you were very young? Maybe it was someone you trust, like your parents or a priest.

Perhaps people believe in their deity for the same reason they speak their native language or walk the way they do. It's simply because it's what they grew up with. It is a belief acquired through interaction with other people in a particular social environment that was formed so early in life that it feels as though it *must* be true.

Chapter 2. What Is Culture?

If you believe the Abrahamic god exists, ask yourself if you would still believe that had you been born in a country not shaped by Abrahamic religions. Odds are you wouldn't. This is not to say that culture is so deterministic that we can't push against prevailing frameworks for belief and action—we can certainly decide to become a Muslim even if we don't grow up in an Islamic nation. But culture is so pervasive, and quietly influential, we often don't even recognize how it shapes our ideas. In most Western countries, the idea that one could be Christian and Muslim at the same time seems strange. They are different religions, despite having the same deity, and the common idea is that religious adherence is exclusive and based on some sort of absolutist belief system. In Japan, this is not how people look at things. In national surveys of religious affiliation, usually about 90 million Japanese describe themselves at Shinto and about 95 million as Buddhist. There are only 120 million Japanese. Additionally, Christian weddings are among the most common in Japan—despite the fact that only about one percent of the population is Christian—largely because people like the aesthetic of what is called a "white wedding" (Edwards, 1989). The reason for this is that for the most part, Japanese do not associate religious behavior with mandatory beliefs, but instead with mandatory rituals. You can believe what you want, but it's important to do certain rituals, particularly when it comes to memorializing ancestors (Traphagan, *The Practice of Concern: Ritual, Well-Being, and Aging in Rural Japan*, 2004).

If you aren't buying this yet, I will give you another, very simple example. Think about counting objects. This seems like a very natural—and non-cultural—thing to do. You have one car, two cars, three cars. Or one dog, two dogs, three dogs. Just pick a number and differentiate between one of the object and more than one. In English, we add an "s" to the word representing the object being counted to identify a difference between singular and plural quantities of that object. Have you ever wondered why we do that? I don't have a clue. It's completely unnecessary. If I write, "I have two dog," you know what I mean. There is no confusion there. In fact, pluralization is so unnecessary that in some languages it is not widely used. Japanese is a good example. The ending *"tachi"* can be used for pluralization, but it is normally used only when it's necessary to differentiate one from many. So, I might write *"watashitachi,"* meaning "us" or "we," to point out that an opinion is not mine alone. When it comes to counting objects, Japanese works very differently from English. Instead of indicating a differentiation between one and more than one of the thing being counted, counting in Japanese involves identifying the size, shape, or function of the object being counted. Table 1 shows how to count some different objects in Japanese.

Table 1. Counting in English and Japanese

Object	*English*	*Japanese*	*Translation*
Dog	One dog, two dogs, three dogs	犬一匹、犬二匹、犬三匹	One (two, three) dog that is a small animal
Car	One car, two cars, three cars	車一台、車2台、車3台	One (two, three) wheeled vehicle that is a machine
Pencil	One pencil, two pencils, three pencils	鉛筆一本、鉛筆2本、鉛筆3本	One (two, three) writing object that is cylindrical
Book	One book, two books, three books	本一冊、本二冊、本三冊	One (two, three) volume that is thick
Paper	One sheet of paper, two sheets of paper, three sheets of paper	髪一枚、髪2枚、髪3枚	One (two, three) paper that is flat and thin

If you look at Table 1 carefully, you will note some significant differences in how Japanese and English speakers count things. As noted, in English, it's important to differentiate one from more than one. This is not important in Japanese. Instead, what matters is identifying the structure of the object being counted. The characters after the numbers (and note you can write numbers either with

Chapter 2. What Is Culture?

kanji characters or with Arabic numerals) are counters, or characters indicating the structure of the object. So 犬一匹 translates literally as "dog one small animal" while 本一冊 translates as "book one volume." There are more than a hundred counters used regularly in Japanese, which can make counting a challenge for non-native speakers of the language.

The point that matters here is not so much that the way we count can differ from one language to another, but that the way we count seems natural to us and the "normal" way anyone would count—until we are confronted with another language that doesn't work that way. If you never learn a foreign language, it is likely that you will go through life believing that counting is unproblematic and is done the same way in all cultures and languages. One of the better humans-meet-aliens movies of all time is *Arrival*, which depicts a linguist trying to communicate with aliens who arrive on Earth in huge, oblong spaceships. At one point the linguist, Louise Banks, explains to her impatient colleagues that the problem isn't simply one of translation, but of thought patterns. She cites something known as the Sapir-Whorf Hypothesis or the theory of linguistic relativity. Sapir-Whorf raises a question about the extent to which language shapes how we think and how our brains model the world.

It has become quite clear from studies of the brain and cognition that the world we experience isn't the "real" world that's out there. Our brains create models of the world using input from our senses. So, when I look out the window from my study and see the ancient red barn and green trees across the street, what I see isn't going to be exactly what you see. If you happen to be color blind, then you will see the objects we are looking at somewhat differently from me. If you happened to be a dog, you would see the colors quite differently (dogs do see color, just not the entire spectrum that humans see). But here's an important observation: Neither of us will see infrared radiation, but it's there. Human eyes don't pick up infrared, so the model of the barn we construct in our heads doesn't include that type of light.

The Myth of Organizational Culture

The models that are constructed in our brains are intimately tied to the specific sensory apparatus our bodies have, and those vary from one organism to another. This relationship is discussed in great detail in one of my favorite books, Bruce Wexler's *Brain and Culture: Neurobiology, Ideology, and Social Change* (Wexler, 2008). Wexler shows how from birth to adulthood our brains use sensory input to develop physically. The specific nature of the stimulation we receive shapes the connections among neurons, which leads to highly varied neural networks in each of our heads that shape behavior. Change the cultural environment and the shapes and structures of our brains develop in different ways. In other words, Japanese don't just count differently from English-speakers. Their brains are wired differently and, as a result, they think about counting—and the world being counted—differently from English-speakers.

This point is so important that I want to bring one more example to bear to hammer it home. I love dogs. They are wonderful beings and incredibly intelligent. Because dogs and humans have co-evolved from at least 10,000 years, we share a great deal. Humans have been selecting traits in dogs that generate connections with humans for a long time. And, yet, if we think for a bit about what it would be like to be a dog, it's clear that the model of the world they create in their heads must be quite different from the models humans create. Why? Because their sensory organs are different. The average human has about 20 million scent receptors in their nose; the average hound dog has ten times that amount. Dog eyes do not see color the same way that human eyes do, and dog ears have a wider spectrum that they can hear in comparison to humans. What this means is that when your dog is going around doing what your dog does, they are processing different information from what you are processing and doing so in a way different from how you do it. The dog has a great deal more input related to scent than you do—so much more it's difficult for humans to imagine what it would be like to experience the world the way dogs do. In fact, dogs get so much information from their noses that they use their noses (rather than their eyes, like humans) to tell

Chapter 2. What Is Culture?

time. No, I'm not making it up. Scientists have been able to explain why dogs know when mom or dad is going to be home prior to their arrival. Throughout the day, dogs measure the scent of their family members and can recognize how the strength of scent is declining throughout the day. They understand that when the scent reaches a particular level, that's about when mom or dad gets home—and they get excited to see their loved one. Unlike the models of the world humans create in their heads, which are highly dependent on visual input, the models dogs create are highly dependent upon olfactory input (Hare & Woods, 2013). This means that their models of reality are different from ours—very different.

Language is part of that complex network of input data that shapes how humans model the world and, thus, different languages lead people to developing different models and different ideas about what the world is normally like. Culture is, too. For a long time, most introductory anthropology textbooks defined culture in ways similar to Pontefract's simple definition: culture is the shared set of implicit and explicit values, ideas, concepts, and rules that guide behavior and allow humans to function in self-perpetuating social groups (Hudelson, 2004). The problem with this type of definition is that it does a poor job of conveying the fact that, like human brains and the physical environment in which they live, culture is dynamic and evolving. It isn't just a set of rules that people buy-in to; it is constantly being socially re-constructed as people interact with each other and interpret the meanings of those rules. It also isn't simplistically located and locatable in things like mission statements. Aspects of a particular cultural context may be *reflected* in things like mission and value statements, but the locus of culture is in the individual minds of the people who come together to form groups and variably make use of cultural artifacts like mission and value statements. Thus, while it may form a sort of social glue that binds people together in some ways, there is a basic empirical question about the extent to which people really share the values, ideas, and interpretations of rules that are associated with a perceived cultural context. When it comes to

The Myth of Organizational Culture

organizations, application of a broad brush-stroke concept of culture tends to have the same problems that it has when applied to complex societies—it glosses over the fact that organizations are conglomerations of various sub-groupings and individuals that can both overlapping interests and ideas, but also can be in conflict. It is not unusual for this to happen simultaneously. An example may be helpful.

I grew up in the Boston area in the 1960s and 1970s. Most of my mother's family was from New Jersey. She came to New England along with my father who was a music professor at the University of Massachusetts Lowell and my Uncle Bob settled in Worcester (I dare you to pronounce that correctly) as a graduate student and then physics professor at Worcester Polytechnic Institute. My grandparents moved to the state to be close to two of their three adult children and their grandchildren. The family had long been Brooklyn Dodgers fans, so much so that the family dog was named Dodger, but they became disillusioned with the team when it traitorously moved to the West Coast in the 1950s along with the Giants. That left only one option of a New York baseball team to follow—the Yankees. But that wasn't possible for Dodgers fans like my family, so they began to follow the Red Sox, which worked out well when the entire clan ended up in Massachusetts.

If you think about it, on the one hand my relatives were both united and divided by their connection to New York City when it came to sports. They followed New York teams, but because the Dodgers and Yankees were enemies, it was easier to switch to the Red Sox when the Dodgers departed for warmer climes. In what ways did the culture unite people around NYC or the Dodgers in this case? In fact, it functioned to divide. This continues in my family right into the present, when it would be sacrilege for anyone to don a Yankees cap. We are all Sox fans and worship at the great shrine of Fenway Park. But, alas, it isn't that simple.

My career took me to a variety of places outside of New England and I ended up settling in Austin, Texas, for a long stretch. I liked Austin, but I don't particularly like Texas. To me living in Austin is

Chapter 2. What Is Culture?

sort of like living in an oasis in the middle of a cesspool—no matter how nice the oasis is, you can still smell the surrounding raw sewage. Identity is closely related to culture and as a result of my distaste for Texas, I have retained a strong sense of being a Massachusetts kid who got stuck living in the southwest due to work. In 2004, my son was playing baseball and as I walked across the complex of diamonds at one of our team's tournaments, I saw another dad whose son had been on a team my son played for the previous years. He, too, was a transplant from New England. The Red Sox had just won the World Series after an 86-year drought—you can play baseball in November in Texas—and as we met, we hugged and nodded in understanding. We didn't say much, because little needed to be said. The culture of being a Red Sox fan and being a New Englander runs deep.

Over the years living in Texas, I've also run across other displaced northerners, several of whom are from New York and also happen to be Yankees fans. Our interactions are complex. On the one hand, if we are watching a ball game together, we are enemies and make it clear that we are from different cultures. Being a Red Sox vs. a Yankees fan isn't just about baseball; it's about Boston vs. New York and the New England mindset vs. the New York mindset. Patriots and Jets fans don't have any more love for each other than Red Sox and Yankees fans (and I don't want to talk about the football Giants who ruined two Superbowls for me). But when we are not watching a ball game, I often find a very comfortable feeling in talking with people from New York. They aren't like Texans and when I talk to them, it feels much more like home. I've been told by people form New York that they often have a similar experience when talking to New Englanders in Texas—it feels like home. Simultaneously, Bostonians and New Yorkers living in Texas can be pulled apart when watching a sporting event and pulled together when talking about things they miss from the northeast or dislike about Texas, such as the dominant conservative political climate. Do we share values? Do we contest values? Are shared political values somehow more important than contested sporting values? Which of these matter more in defining one's cultural identity? How do we make sense out of this behavior when talking about culture as some sort of glue that binds people in social groups together? Lots of questions.

One of the more significant problems with the culture concept is that it tends to generate a sense of boundedness that does not reflect empirical reality. In an article titled "What Is Culture?" for the website LiveScience (October 17, 2022), Callum McKelvie and Stephanie Pappas gives some examples of how we typically use the term culture when applied to national and international frames of experience.

> Eastern culture generally refers to the societal norms of countries in Far East Asia (including China, Japan, Vietnam, North Korea and South Korea) and the Indian subcontinent. Like the West, Eastern culture was heavily influenced by religion during its early development, but it was also heavily influenced by the growth and harvesting of rice, according to the book *Pathways to Asian Civilizations: Tracing the Origins and Spread of Rice and Rice Cultures* by Dorian Q. Fuller. In general, in Eastern culture there is less of a distinction between secular society and religious philosophy than there is in the West.

This paragraph nicely captures the problem with talking about culture. "Eastern culture" is actually meaningless. While there are some commonalities across the countries mentioned—such as rice agriculture and the influence of Confucianism among some, but not all—this explanation completely covers over the considerable variation that exists among, and within, these societies. For example, the People's Republic of China (PRC), the Koreas, and Japan all share an influence from Chinese Confucianism, but one must keep in mind that localized interpretations of Confucianism arose in societies outside of China as well as within China over the centuries (Murayama, 1975) (Ro, 2021). North Korea is a communist dictatorship, the PRC is a capitalist dictatorship, South Korea and Japan are capitalist democracies. People living in North Korea are socialized through education and propaganda into seeing Japan as an enemy, not as a country with a common cultural background. If you think about it for a moment, it is highly unlikely that much is actually shared among these societies. In fact, the idea of "Eastern" culture is really a

Chapter 2. What Is Culture?

product of ethnocentrism and imperialism, both from Western societies and also from Japan, which attempted to create a sense of East Asian culture in its Greater East Asian Coprosperity Sphere, which was just a long name for the Japanese Empire. And, what is Asia anyway? Asia is a largely meaningless concept—it includes Afghanistan, India, Vietnam, Japan, etc. Depending on the source, it extends into the Middle East and can include Iran. From a cultural perspective, there is little reason to think that these countries share a great deal and the conceptualization of "Asia" as a place with some sort of common cultural, racial, or ethnic element is a product of the imaginations of Western imperialists. As the scholar Edward Said put it when discussing his book *Orientalism*, "I emphasize in it [my Orientalism] accordingly that neither the term Orient nor the concept of the West has any ontological stability; each is made up of human effort, partly affirmation, partly identification of the Other" (goodreads.com).

Asia was something defined as Other to those societies, like England, who were engaged in imperialism. It has no real value as a concept that reflects much of anything about culture, because the cultures it encapsulates are so diverse as to lend little credence to the notion that they necessarily share much. Early in my career when I first started teaching at Cal State Fullerton, I was told to teach a course they had on the books called Peoples of Asia. I had no idea what to do, so I spent the first two weeks deconstructing the idea of Asia and the notion that it is a meaningful way to think about any particular "peoples." Terms that connote commonality across vast cultural and geographical regions, like Asia, tend to do more damage than good. They cover over the complex variations in behavior, values, and ideas that exist within any region so defined. Even within a country, like Japan, which is often (erroneously) represented as homogeneous, cultural variation is extensive (Robertson, 2018). In standard Japanese, the word for "yes" is "*hai.*" But if you go to the region where I do ethnographic fieldwork, you will find that not only do people say "*hai*" to affirm things, but also sometimes say "*ndanda.*" It's a word from a local dialect and represents

The Myth of Organizational Culture

the tip of the iceberg when it comes to the fact that many locals speak in ways distinct from standard Japanese. The dialect is so different from standard Japanese that people from Tokyo often have difficulties understanding locals—particularly older people—despite the fact that they are speaking the same language.

The way of defining culture I have been exploring, and critiquing, in this chapter tends to present it as a coherent thing that can somehow be found objectively in the world. It represents culture as having neat boundaries and people who live within those boundaries as having clearly established, uncontested values that they unambiguously share. This model assumes that people largely conform to expectations and behaviors associated with that particular culture. In organizational culture tomes, there is often the belief that things like mission statements help in generating this assumed conformity. Often, physical objects are taken as representative of a culture or as tools for generating a sense of cultural unity. Think of coffee mugs or t-shirts with the corporate logo on them. When it comes to larger contexts, we also often use objects as a way to somehow encapsulate a culture. Kimono or sushi in Japan. Fish and chips in the UK. But there's a problem. Sushi is not only Japanese. California roll was developed in North America, but you can get it in other countries, too. In fact, California roll has found its way back to Japan and it has been further innovated as Japanese find interesting ways to incorporate avocado and other new ingredients into their own take on sushi.

This brings us to the problem of what we mean when we talk about organizational culture. When it comes to an organization, is culture found in mission and value statements? Is it found in the arrangement of cubicles? Is it in the type of paperclips we use? In some ways, it's reflected in all these things and more, but you can't easily grab it and control it. It's like the old Buddhist saying about holding a handful of sand; the harder you squeeze the more sand slips through your fingers. What does it mean to talk about an organizational "culture" when the people who work in the organization come from different backgrounds, ethnicities, genders, and cultural

Chapter 2. What Is Culture?

contexts and, hence, have brains that are constructed in different ways as a result of growing up in those cultural contexts and learning different languages or different ways of seeing the world?

In their book, *Designing Exceptional Organizational Cultures: How to Develop Companies Where Employees Thrive,* Jacobs and Crockett present an exceptional example of this way of thinking about culture. The authors write:

> Our definition revolves around values and accepted behaviors that are demonstrated through *everyone's* actions. These are what drive a company's culture.... Your culture is what creates that special sauce that makes your organization unique; it's the DNA that makes you special and stand out from the rest.... Culture is formed by the interactions people have with one another. Culture is what happens when actions, behaviors, and values intersect... [Jacobs & Crockett, 2021, 10] [emphasis added].

There we go again with the special sauce trope. This definition is remarkable for the way it circles back on itself and shows a deep lack of understanding about how culture works. The last two sentences are right on the mark, culture involves interactions among people and arises when actions and values intersect. The problem is with the first sentence: it is extremely unlikely that in any organization *everyone* will orient their behaviors around a set of values established by upper managers or anyone else. People *interpret* the values that are presented to them. They don't just line up and follow whatever is posted on a mission or values statement. In the process of interpreting values, they bring their own ideas to the table. A person who was raised in a different country, for example, may interpret the values of an organization in a very different way from the person sitting in the cubicle next to her. Someone who is Queer may think about those values in very different ways from someone who is a cis white male. In other words, individuals will neither uncritically accept nor unambiguously demonstrate common values *in any organization*, because each person brings their own life history to the ways in which they interpret and demonstrate those values. Let me emphasize this: *Because people have different brain structures*

The Myth of Organizational Culture

*and life experiences it is **not possible** for everyone in an organization to accept, adhere to, or demonstrate commitment to common values unconditionally.*

This problem was driven home for me a few years ago, when I gave a lecture on ethics and culture for the facilities service managers at my university. We talked about the mission statement and core values of the University of Texas at Austin. The university website posts them for everyone to read:

Mission

The mission of The University of Texas at Austin is to achieve excellence in the interrelated areas of undergraduate education, graduate education, research and public service. The university provides superior and comprehensive educational opportunities at the baccalaureate through doctoral and special professional educational levels.

The university contributes to the advancement of society through research, creative activity, scholarly inquiry and the development and dissemination of new knowledge, including the commercialization of University discoveries. The university preserves and promotes the arts, benefits the state's economy, serves the citizens through public programs and provides other public service.

Core Purpose

To transform lives for the benefit of society.

Core Values

Learning—A caring community, all of us students, helping one another grow.

Discovery—Expanding knowledge and human understanding.

Freedom—To seek the truth and express it.

Leadership—The will to excel with integrity and the spirit that nothing is impossible.

Individual Opportunity—Many options, diverse people and ideas, one university.

Responsibility—To serve as a catalyst for positive change in Texas and beyond.

I asked the managers to form groups and discuss the mission and value statements presented by the organization for which they

Chapter 2. What Is Culture?

worked. Some interesting responses arose in our discussion. First, all of the managers indicated that they feel the ways in which the values, purpose, and mission statements are presented basically ignores the importance of facilities maintenance—excellence in facilities maintenance is clearly not part of the mission presented in the statement. In other words, these managers felt left out of the mission being presented by university leaders. Everything in these statements is quite abstract—probably exactly what one would expect from the professors who wrote them. But if you think about it for a moment, well-maintained facilities are central to the educational mission of any institution. In fact, as a public university, those facilities belong to the citizens of the state and, as such, are a key component of their investment in quality higher education and research. As we discussed these statements, it became clear that the managers in the room largely believed that their work is a fundamental component in the *educational* mission of the university—but they don't think the mission/purpose/values statements reflect any awareness among leadership of that idea. As we unpacked the implications of the mission and values statements of the university, the conversation turned to the symbolic messages that were sent by the university in relation to facilities maintenance. For example, some of the participants noted that the buildings associated with facilities maintenance are at the outermost periphery of the campus. They are so remote, that one has to cross a major Interstate simply to get to their buildings, which is beyond the edge of what most people actually think of as the campus.

As we talked about the relationship of employees who work in facilities to the rest of the university, an interesting theme arose—they see themselves as left out of the primary mission of the university. Now, as you think about this, ask yourself to what extent managers and others working in facilities maintenance at the University of Texas feel bound together in a common culture of excellence expressed in the mission and value statements presented on the organizational website? In fact, those exact statements,

The Myth of Organizational Culture

particularly when combined with things like the physical remoteness from the main campus, generate feelings of isolation and even alienation from the mission—and perceived culture—of the university. The managers I spoke with felt entirely left out of the educational and research mission stated by leaders, but at the same time also felt like what they do is fundamentally important to that mission. In short, the mission and value statements were sources of conflict, not community.

Another version of the seminar I taught at a museum had a similar outcome. The museum's mission statement hit all the right buzzwords: leadership, excellence, diversity, engagement, etc., and described the museum as a steward of the knowledge and history displayed in its collection with the aim of making these things accessible to people of all ages. The seminar included managers from all departments in the museum, and everyone agreed that this idea of stewardship mattered. But when we discussed the overall challenges the museum was facing, I learned that there was a sharp division between those who worked on the upper floors—the administrators and curators who ran the show—and the people who worked on the lower floors meeting guests, selling tickets, and taking care of the maintenance of the building. As we discussed the mission statement, I was told by the managers of the people who work on the lower decks that they didn't feel the statement reflected their contributions, nor the importance of those who are on the front lines of helping the people who visit. They noted that the museum had a clear class and status hierarchy, evident in the division between employees of the upper floors (leadership) and those of the lower floors (workers).

The tension in the room became rapidly quite palpable when this conversation emerged—they all knew there was a problem but had not realized that the problem was itself seen as being reflected in the mission statement. In fact, the upper-floor managers had not conceptualized the tensions that existed in the organization in terms of social stratification evident in the structure of the organization

Chapter 2. What Is Culture?

and which was reflected in the writing of the mission statement. I was left wondering about this a bit, however, because the museum's director, when asked prior to the seminar to provide a copy of the mission statement so that we could discuss it in the class, she refused to do so. Fortunately, she hadn't realized that said mission statement was framed and easily visible hanging on the wall of the conference room where we met.

It doesn't matter who was right in either of these examples. Perhaps when the mission statements were written by high-level managers or directors, they were thinking about the maintenance staff, security personnel, and cashiers who work at these institutions. What does matter is that—regardless of intent—the same exact mission statements were interpreted in drastically different ways by members of the organizations who had different roles within the organizations. I think it would be reasonable to assume that all mission statements are subject to varied interpretation. It is highly unlikely that one can get a group of people together—with different ethnic, racial, gendered, aged, and who inhabit different social spaces with different experiences—who will interpret a statement or even the meanings of words like leadership in the same way. Humans simply bring too much baggage with them based on their experiences in life to arrive at the same, or in many cases even similar, interpretations.

One last example: A few years ago, faculty at my university received a message that the administration wanted us to go to the football stadium wearing burnt orange (our school color) so that we could make a huge human representation of our university logo for a photo shoot. Some faculty—particularly administrators—are gung-ho about the university and wear burnt orange ties or sport jackets to every event, but many faculty have mixed feelings about university leadership, the overwhelming prominence of the athletic department on campus, and are not necessarily interested in the sporting efforts of the school. Many, like me, don't wear burnt orange and don't become much involved in the whole school spirit

The Myth of Organizational Culture

thing—we are employees focused on education and research. Many faculty resisted and refused to participate, in some cases scoffing or laughing at the effort. Clearly, as I heard one colleague state, administrators have no concept of how faculty perceive of their identities on campus! There was some surprise at the negative response and I'm not sure whether the photo shoot happened. Interestingly, when a colleague posted on Facebook about how silly she thought the request was, a former student was shocked and annoyed because he had always assumed faculty were just as wrapped up in school spirit as students.

People *always* interpret their surroundings and act in ways that blend their own ideas with those being presented to them. How one constructs a sense of self-identity and how one views the ascription of identity to oneself by others matters. If you think about an organization the size of the University of Texas at Austin—with 80,000 students, faculty and staff, many of whom were raised outside of Texas and outside of the United States—the idea of an organizational culture defined as a socially unifying set of mission and value statements makes no sense. When Jacobs and Crockett describe culture as "the ecosystem of any organization" they do recognize that how culture "is viewed can differ depending on your lens," but that's not exactly the problem (Jacobs & Crockett, 2021, 11). The values themselves are interpreted and constructed differently depending on your cultural lens—each of us brings a particular set of personal and cultural constructs to the interpretation of anything we encounter. This is much more profound than just some differences depending on what color sunglasses you happen to be wearing. Culture, if it really exists as a thing, is a set ideas and values that live in *individual* minds. These ideas and values are based on personal interpretations of how things should and should not be done in a social environment. They rely on what people consider to be true and false. Therefore, they can vary a lot from one person to another because, going back to Wexler's ideas, people brains are shaped by cultural context. It's not that we are just wearing different glasses; it's that our brains

Chapter 2. What Is Culture?

interpret what is seen in sometimes vastly different ways. Culture isn't about "common values" but about how people interpret values treated *as though* they are agreed upon by members of a group. But it is important to recognize that simply because a set of values are treated *as though* they are held in common, it's not necessarily the case that everyone affected by those values thinks about them in the same, or even similar, ways.

In fact, people routinely contest the values expressed as though they are held in common by leaders of an organization. They may do this through open disagreement or through more subtle means such as altering their work patterns or taking more sick days. This shapes the social environment and becomes part of a social performance or play that can be overtly expressed or tacitly acted out, observed, and interpreted. Normally, it's a combination of these. If you work from the idea that mission and value statements will bring people together and encourage teamwork, there is a very good chance you will be surprised at some point to find out that it didn't work out that way. In other words, the idea that mission and value statements generate a common organizational culture is delusional, because there is simply too much diversity within any organization for that to actually happen.

CULTURE IS A COMPLEX CONCEPT

So back to the question, "What (the hell) is culture?" If it's so messy, is there any point in talking about it at all? Although I do think the culture concept has value, we need to be careful about how we use the term. In my research related to the culture concept, I have come to think of it as a *process* rather than as a *property* of groups. People not only are held together, but may be divided by their customs and beliefs, values, and mission statements—even when they ostensibly belong to the same "culture" or organization. Rather than a deterministic "thing" with identifiable boundaries and consistently received messages that are uncontested and uninterpreted, culture is better understood as a process by which people continually create, accept, contest and reinvent the customs, beliefs, and ideas that they use—collectively, individually, and often strategically—to characterize their surroundings.

Figure 1 represents one way to think about this process as a cycle in which people interpret values, actions, and beliefs or ideas. Note that it is not unidirectional—the flow of the process is multi-directional and at the core of what happens with values, actions and beliefs/ideas is the subprocess of interpretation. One's values influence how one acts or the ideas one has; but the ideas one has and the actions one takes also influence the process of interpretation. This process, of course, does not happen in isolation, because we not only interpret our own actions and ideas, but those of others, as well. When thinking about ideas, interpretations, values, etc., collectively, I use the term *construct*, borrowing from the work of philosopher and physicist Henry Margenau (Margenau, 1961). By constructs I mean abstractions that humans use to make sense of their world and to *construct* or build models of the world in their heads. This is synonymous with the word concept but emphasizes the fact that these abstractions are things humans make and use to interpret the world. When I look at the magnolia tree in my front yard, I am not seeing the tree as it is—I am seeing it as my brain constructs it, which is a product of a complex interaction of my sensing of the physical world and the cultural structures that have shaped how I interpret that world. I don't experience the tree objectively in part because my sensory organs are not able to access all of the different ways in which the tree exists. For example, I don't see the trace amounts of radioactive elements like potassium-40 that all living things contain and that the tree emits. We can also ask if I see the tree as beautiful because it is objectively so or because I live in a cultural context in which magnolia trees are seen as beautiful? Not all flowers are viewed equally—think about the poor, lowly dandelion. It seems to me a lovely flower, but Americans go to great effort and expense

Chapter 2. What Is Culture?

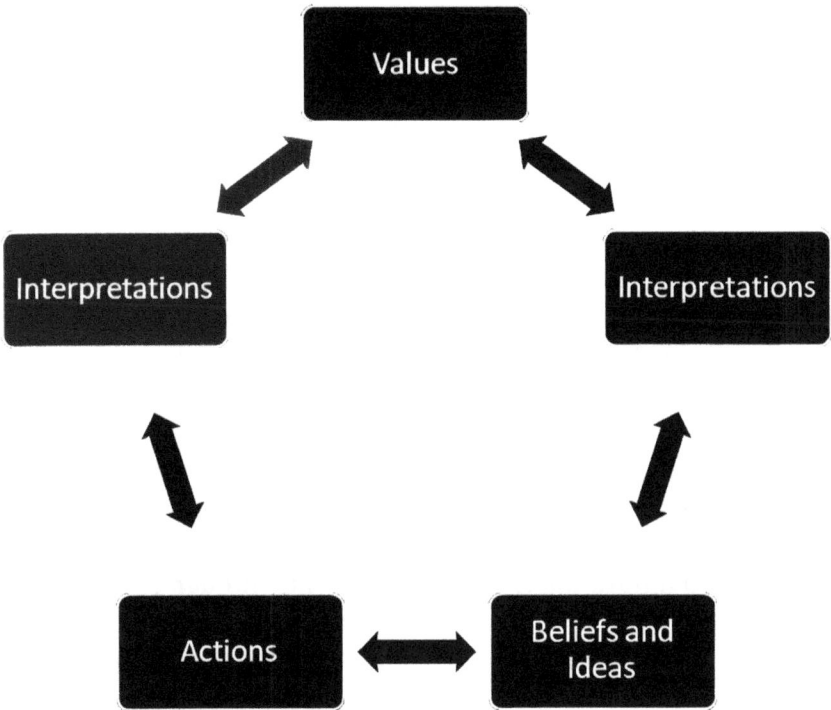

Figure 1. Culture understood as a cyclical process in which interpretations influence values and actions.

to irradicate dandelions from their laws because they see them as weeds and, thus, not aesthetically pleasing.

In other words, the tree—as constructed in my head—is a complex intertwining of the physical object, what my body can interpret of the physical object, and the ways in which my culture and language influence how I ascribe meaning to that object. And this is not static. The ways in which these elements of experience interact changes over time. What a tree means to me today will change if tomorrow a tree falls on me and breaks my leg. It may shift from being interpreted as an object of beauty to one of fear or angst. Culture is not a state or condition—it is a concept used to represent a dynamic cascading system in which there is a constant

The Myth of Organizational Culture

transfer and interpretation of ideas and actions along a network of component sub-systems (all aspects of the physical world that our individual brains experience and construct models of) which generate output that constantly becomes the input for adjacent subsystems that are engaged in interpreting input and generating output.

People enact this process much like the way jazz musicians read what is known as a lead sheet. For those less versed in musical vernacular, a lead sheet is a way of writing music that only involves presenting the melody and the chords that should be played while one is performing the piece. These chords are called changes, because they change as one moves through the melodic structure of the tune. When a jazz musician reads a lead sheet, she usually first plays the tune largely straight—without much improvisation—and then during solos begins to improvise, which involves taking the changes and the melody and innovating these into new forms through the embodied action of playing the instrument. The basic melodic and harmonic structure of the tune will remain largely the same and often can be heard during the solos, although a good jazz musician may veer very far away from that structure in the process of creating and expressing innovative and original ideas. However, if the musician deviates too far from the basic form of the tune, either in terms of the melody or the changes, it may become difficult for the listener to interpret—it loses its internal logic and, thus, does not really make sense in relation to the form and structure of the tune being performed. Part of what makes a great jazz musician, like Thelonious Monk or Charlie Parker, is the ability to deviate significantly from the melody or changes—to create novel interpretations (constructs)—while staying enough within the parameters outlined in the lead sheet so that the song continues to make sense to listeners. The structure evident in the lead sheet may be interpretively stretched considerably, but the good jazz musician is able to work the changes and melody in such a way that eventually she finds her way back to the original structure. I would argue that the core of what makes jazz interesting and what

Chapter 2. What Is Culture?

generates art is experiencing how musician expresses their musical ideas and innovate while staying to some extent within the form or context of each tune.

The cascade system that is culture works in largely the same way. The discourses and tropes that we associate with or that are employed in a particular cultural context operate like a lead sheet—the rules, values, statements that identify the boundaries in which behavior is considered normal. These things give our experiences form or structure that allow us to interpret what is going on around us. In other words, culture is about expectations. One's identity as a cultural being is comprised of expectations about what one should do, who one should be, and who one wants to be and how others interpret those things. These are drawn from or based upon social and ideological conceptual frameworks that define the limits of how we think about behavior within a particular group of people. When expectations are expressed through actions, they have a kind of automatic quality to them that we often identify as being natural. Expectations are so deeply ingrained that people often don't notice that they even have them. By doing what you are expected to do, you begin, yourself, to expect a specific type of behavior and treat certain behaviors as unambiguously natural and normal.

Culture unfolds in the expectations of individuals, which are patterned in a given society to help people navigate their interactions with others, who often have similar expectations. If you are an American, you might now be thinking, "my expectations are entirely unlike those of the opposing political party." The U.S. is a rather bifurcated society politically right now. But, believe it or not, conservatives and liberals share many expectations that are products of American culture. They expect to be able to voice their opinions and to be heard. They expect a society that is just and in which the economy works to support their needs. They expect to be able to find work and to live comfortably. Of course, Americans can differ significantly on how to attain those expectations

The Myth of Organizational Culture

and that leads to conflict. The cultural context in the U.S. generates a structure in which people share many types of expectations but can also be strongly opposed in how to meet those expectations. That context can both unite and divide people at the same time.

Expectations are constantly being negotiated and improvised upon and sometimes the process of negotiation and improvisation can cause root changes in one's expectational patterns. When behaviors of others fall outside of the patterns of expectations, then one is forced to react in order to organize those observed behaviors into a way that fits into the range of acceptable expectations operating in a given cultural context. This response, a kind of improvisation, may include adjustment of one's own expectations or generate interpersonal conflict as one attempts to modify the expectations and behaviors of others. The boundaries of any culture are permeable and are constantly being interpreted and innovated upon by the individuals within a context. If one pushes the edges of those interpretive structures too far, they stop making sense and people have difficulties interpreting and understanding behaviors. In other words, innovative expressions of ideas and behaviors that are too far outside the structure of the changes or melody—the value structures and practices—associated with a given cultural context create difficulties in interpreting their meanings.

Any social performance is constantly changing, because those in charge of setting the tone of the performance (or culture, if we want to call it that) and those who follow leadership react to the behaviors and expressions of each other. At one level, everyone is involved in continuously setting that tone and direction, because the entire context operates as a kind of feedback loop in which the ideas and actions of one individual shape those of others. This happens both vertically and horizontally and is the reason why change is a constant.

Chapter 2. What Is Culture?

Key Takeaways

- *Culture is hard to pinpoint and define.*
- *Culture is about change. It's not a thing; it's a process.*
- *Culture can divide as much as it can unify and can do both at the same time.*
- *Culture cannot be easily engineered.*

CHAPTER 3

Why Organizations Don't Have Cultures

Before DEC collapsed, I moved on to a small company that wrote software for the food distribution industry. They hired me because I worked at DEC and they thought I could bring my experience as a technical editor and writer to help clean up their disastrously bad software manuals. When I opened one of their manuals during my interview, I had to hold back the laughter. It amazed me that anyone could use their software having read the manual. It was filled with typos, poorly constructed instructions, and unintelligible sentences. They offered me a good raise, so I took the job and moved down from Massachusetts to Long Island. I learned later on that they considered firing me after two weeks because I wasn't fixing their software manuals quickly enough. Their expectations were a tad absurd, given how bad their software manuals were, but that didn't matter. It needed to get done. Of course, it was precisely that attitude that had led to crappy software manuals and, in fact, crappy software.

The company had no espoused values of which I was aware and I had never seen anything like a mission statement. But this was also a time before the mission and value statement craze had taken hold in much of the business world, so that isn't surprising. To be honest, it wasn't much fun working at that company. The only thing that seemed to motivate corporate leaders was making money. That was the organizational paradigm. Sell the software and make money. They didn't care much about quality, ethics, or values. They didn't even seem to care if the software worked—and it often didn't. I hated

Chapter 3. Why Organizations Don't Have Cultures

the environment and disliked the management intensely. But the job paid the bills and helped me decide to go back to graduate school to become an anthropologist.

Much of what happened at that company reflected broader 1980s-style cultural values and archetypes of success—the "greed is good" model of business. In fact, that phrase would be a good way to sum-up their organizational paradigm, which involved a clearly evident process that repeated itself several times while I worked there and was the basic mode of operation that characterized much of what happened at the company in terms of sales and software development. This is how it worked. First, sales representatives would convince a prospective client (we will call the company Supply and Packing Systems, Inc. or SAPS) that the software—very expensive software selling at about one million dollars way back in 1989—had a variety of features that would allow SAPS' warehouses to run more efficiently. Second, SAPS would pay my company (we will call it Remote American Technology Systems, Inc. or RATS) a ton of money. At this point, RATS would hire a group of temporary developers to work furiously for several weeks because, in fact, the software didn't actually do what RATS told SAPS it would do. Most of the time, it wasn't even close. Of course, the new code was full of bugs so when RATS installed their newly coded software on SAPS' computers, it wouldn't work. RATS would then explain that the software needed to be "customized" to SAPS' hardware, therefore it would be necessary to bring in software consultants—at the expense of SAPS—to get the software to work on SAPS' hardware systems. In short, RATS would charge companies like SAPS not only for the software they were purchasing (that didn't quite exist when being purchased), but also to debug the code created for the functions they had lied about when selling the package.

I suspect many who read the above description, but probably not all, would view the sales practices of RATS as unethical. I certainly did and left the company as soon as I could. I literally kicked my heels when I walked out the door on my last day. But the reality of

The Myth of Organizational Culture

RATS' potential moral failing is more complex. For one thing, ethical business practices were not defined the same way in 1989 that they are today. In fact, the Society for Business Ethics had only been formed nine years earlier and academic discussions of business ethics emerged a few years earlier in the 1970s (DeGeorge, 2015). Much of this was in response to corporate behaviors that seemed to show little concern for ethics at all, particular in the auto industry. One good example was Ralph Nader's attack on the first-generation Chevrolet Corvair. My father came to hate Nader, because he loved his 1966 Corvair. Nader had written a book, *Unsafe at Any Speed*, that pointed out handling issues in the rear-engine, swing axel design GM had developed and which could lead to loss of rear wheel grip and oversteer. A front anti-roll bar would have addressed the problem and GM engineers advocated for it, but management rejected the idea, which would have added production costs. By the time my father bought his Corvair, GM had corrected the suspension issues and incorporated other improvements to the car. But Nader's writing doomed the Corvair and contributed to the creation of a negative image of Detroit auto makers. This was amplified a few years later when Ford designed the Pinto, built from 1971 through 1980. The Pinto was a subcompact intended to compete with the surge of Japanese small cars that had become popular following the rapid increase in gas prices in the early 1970s. The car was reasonably priced and looked okay, but it had one minor flaw that tended to reduce some of its utility as a vehicle. It tended to explode when hit from behind, even at low speed. From an ethics standpoint, one might argue that engineering errors happen and the main moral issue is that they get resolved quickly, particularly if they are a safety hazard. However, Ford knew the Pinto tended to catch fire even as a result of low-speed rear collisions and fuel leakage and they considered a variety of fixes to the problem. They rejected all of them, as Motor Trend Magazine notes, because "they would have added cost and put the program behind schedule" (Gold, 2024).

It might seem obvious in the mid–2020s that a design flaw like

Chapter 3. Why Organizations Don't Have Cultures

this needed to be fixed immediately, but Ford saw things a bit differently in part due to a broader social atmosphere that did not necessarily define Ford's approach as unethical—it's doubtful (to me, at least) that executives at Ford saw what they were doing as unethical at the time they made the decision, even if from our perspective we think they should have. Perhaps they did after several people were killed in Pinto fires. I have no idea. I would hope so, but in reality the situation is culturally complex, because the U.S. Federal government didn't have standards in place requiring cars to withstand a low-speed rear impact without fuel leakage until the 1977 model year. Later Pintos were modified to address this change in standards and old Pintos that had adhered to the prior regulatory context were retrofitted with the safter design. On top of the lack of regulations that might have prevented the issue, while the National Traffic and Highway Safety Administration (NTHSA) estimated about 27 people had died in fiery Pinto crashes, the magazine *Mother Jones* published an article that estimated at least 500 people had been killed and speculated the number might be as high as 900 (Dowie, 1977). The Pinto predicament arose in a climate of limited government safety regulations, a corporate environment that emphasized profits and an attempt to keep the price of the car low (in a period of high inflation, particularly for gas prices), and a media environment that tended to sensationalize the failings of corporate and governmental America (remember Nixon's Watergate scandal emerged in 1972, leading to his resignation in 1974, which generated considerable mistrust in governmental and other organizations). Where, exactly, do we place moral culpability in this complex and changing environment? It's easy to place the blame on Ford, but the company was operating within a particular cultural and regulatory context that shaped its own organizational paradigm. If we blame Ford alone, or Ford's leadership alone, we are basically saying they are culpable for behaving in a way consistent with the cultural context in which they lived and that shaped their organizational paradigm. Also, keep in mind that there are plenty of other aspects of car design that have been dangerous, but that were not a focus of public attention. In the 1950s, prior to the development of retracting steering columns, it was common for drivers to be impaled by the steering column in a crash. I doubt car manufacturers were unaware of this. There were also no regulations preventing it. Who is to blame from a moral perspective?

We need to be careful in jumping to conclusions about what is and what is not ethical. Context matters and the larger cultural and business context of the 1980s in which RATS was operating didn't necessarily squelch this kind of behavior. That doesn't mean it was ethical, nor that people couldn't see the problems with the approach RATS took—I did, as did others in the company. The executives at RATS who promoted this approach were, in my view, pretty slimy, but they were also behaving in a way not inconsistent with the business context of the time. The Pinto debacle seems fairly clear-cut, but the decisions of Ford's executives should be placed in the context of the regulatory environment of the time, which did not require the issue to be addressed. It's also important to recognize that the extent of Pinto dangers was sensationalized in the media. I'm not defending Ford and, in fact, think their decision to enter production while knowing of the danger was unethical, as was their decision to refrain from fixing the problem until 1977, at which time regulations changed and they retrofit older Pintos with the fixes developed for the 1977 model year. But they were not required to address the problem under the regulatory environment in which they were operating at the time. So, who do we blame? Ford? NHTSA? Congress?

The case of the Corvair is more complicated. For one thing, the suspension system GM used was similar to that found in other rear-engine cars, such as the VW Bug and some Porsches—thus it was not an odd approach or unusual technology being used without precedence. Also, a debate emerged about how problematic the handling was that continues even today. In an interesting YouTube video, Larry Webster drives an unmodified 1962 Corvair to find out

Chapter 3. Why Organizations Don't Have Cultures

just how dangerous the handling was. He concludes that the car's handling characteristics were *different* from most cars of the time, but they were not worse nor more dangerous. This meant that there was some risk in average drivers not fully grasping how to respond to the driving characteristics of the car, which could, in fact, lead to a roll. But other cars have similar handling characteristics and in Webster's video engineers involved with the design of the car argue that the car was engineered to be inexpensive, thus it had a simple suspension system—not a *flawed* one.

Some Corvair enthusiasts, like my father, came to view Nader as a nutty zealot who killed a good car largely for personal gain while throwing Corvair enthusiasts into the nadir of automotive Hell. *Car and Driver* columnist Brock Yates went so far as to put Nader into a group he referred to as "Safety Nazis" intent upon making cars boring (Webster, 2017). Indeed, Nader's book contributed to the creation of emissions and safety regulations that hindered performance in the early 1970s. My dad traded his beloved Corvair for something with a little more oomph—a 1968 Pontiac GTO. Frankly, I'm not sure he was qualified to drive a car with a 400 cubic inch engine and 350 horsepower, but he loved "Ralph" even while my mother often complained that GTO stood for Gas, Tune-ups, and Oil. I do remember my father being thrilled when the car managed more than 10 miles per gallon on a tank of gas. A reasonable question would be whether that 1968 GTO, given its performance specs and poor handling characteristics, was any more dangerous than the 1966 Corvair he traded-in for it as a result of the anti–Corvair atmosphere that emerged following Nader's book. It certainly was, according to my father, much more difficult to drive in the winter than the Corvair had been, with its rear-engine and rear-drive set-up, providing good traction unlike the GTO.

Between writers like Nader questioning the safety of what Detroit was producing and the OPEC oil embargo, the era of cool muscle cars gave way to a period of boring econoboxes like the (itself rather flawed) Chevy Vega, Honda Civic, and AMC Gremlin, along with a national 55-mph speed limit to reduce gas consumption and make roads safer. The context in which companies like Ford and GM were doing business had changed and the products they made, as well as their approach to safety, needed to change as well—the organizational paradigms for these companies needed to address the changing cultural climate in which they operated. And, in fact, American automakers struggled with this change, producing some monumentally bad cars, like the Cadillac Cimarron, while trying to compete with Japanese automakers whose organizational paradigms were far better aligned with larger cultural and economic tendencies of that time.

Tacit Value Systems

The question these examples raise is simple: Were the failures of Ford, GM, and RATS the product of bad organizational "cultures?" They were certainly the result of some poor decision-making of questionable ethical merit, but decisions don't happen in a social vacuum. They usually reflect something about the context in which they are made—in these cases not only the organizational context, but the larger cultural context in which the managers were operating at the time. When we talk about ethics, we necessarily must talk about values—our ethical systems are grounded in the social and cultural values in which we make decisions (Traphagan J.W., 2013). At the time these decisions were made, changing value systems were reflected in changing regulations related to automotive safety and, perhaps rather slowly, corporations like Ford and GM adjusted. Keep in mind that in the 1950s safety features were not particularly central to automotive sales—seatbelts did not become available on most U.S. cars until the late 1950s and they were usually options, rather than standard equipment, at first. Today, all states, with the exception of New Hampshire, have mandatory seat belt laws. Things change. As for RATS, the behavior of the corporate leadership was, frankly, pretty

Chapter 3. Why Organizations Don't Have Cultures

gross, but it also reflected a money-first attitude that was common in the 1980s.

We can rephrase this issue to capture something of problem of cultural change: Were the decisions by Ford and GM executives products of bad organizational cultures or were they reflections of changing cultural values in which safety had yet to become a dominant value among automotive buyers? To ask this question is to also ask another important question: to what extent do the ways organizations operate reflect value structures found in the societies in which they operate? Answers to these questions require thinking about the relationship between organizations and larger cultural and social contexts. And the place to start in thinking about this is to focus on values.

Let's begin that investigation by returning to the core values of the university I worked at for many years, where the missions and values web page (https://www.utexas.edu/about/mission-and-values) states that the "core values of The University of Texas at Austin are learning, discovery, freedom, leadership, individual opportunity, and responsibility." These are what we might call overt values, expressed by leadership and intended to convey a sense of how they (leaders) see the organization and the ideals that individuals connected to the university should individually and collectively exhibit. There is nothing wrong with this, even if, as I discussed earlier in the book, these ideals are likely to be interpreted quite differently among members of the university community. We'll set that problem aside for now and instead focus on a different question: Are there other values not expressed in this statement that matter to the organization and to its leaders?

The answer is yes. In fact, there are quite a few of them. Some examples might be maintenance of organizational hierarchy, deference to authority, competition, gender bias related to leadership, and money. I know, you are thinking, "he's rather cynical." I am, but that's not the motivation behind identifying these values as important to the organization. We can see how some of these values exist

The Myth of Organizational Culture

by drawing a comparison. In my post-retirement life, I've come to spend a great deal of time working for my alma mater, the University of Massachusetts Lowell. One of the things I've noticed is that the tacit value structures of UML and UT are quite different. We can see this in both the people selected as leaders and in how leadership interacts with the larger organizational community. Let's begins with a fact. Since its founding in 1883, the University of Texas at Austin has had thirty presidents. Every one of them has been a white, male probably cisgendered, although throughout most of the university's history—reflecting broader social trends—gender and sexual orientation weren't discussed. Over 140 years, there has never been a woman president of the university, nor a person of color. The only diversity of which I am aware among UT presidents can be found in the 29th president, Gregory Fenves, who is Jewish. The history of UML is more complex, due to its being the product of a merger between Lowell Technological Institute and Lowell State College in the 1970s, but the historical pattern of leadership isn't much different from UT. Until recently. The past two chancellors of the University of Massachusetts Lowell have been women, including the current holder of the position, Julie Chen, who identifies as LGBTQ+ and is a woman of Asian descent.

There is clearly something different in how decisions about university leadership are being made in Texas and Massachusetts. The Board of Regents in Texas has been very conservative in selecting leaders for the state's flagship university, although women have served as presidents at a few other UT campuses. Of the ten members of the UT Board of Regents, two are women and one is a person of color (male) as of this writing. Of the twenty-two members of the Massachusetts Higher Education Board of Trustees, eight are women and at least six are people of color. The point here is that decisions about who inhabits leadership positions reflect the values operating in particular social and cultural contexts. The easy way to explain this difference between Massachusetts and Texas is to simply note that the two states are significantly dissimilar in terms of

Chapter 3. Why Organizations Don't Have Cultures

their political leanings, with Massachusetts being on the liberal side and Texas on the conservative side which also reflects things like attitudes and values related to gender, race, and leadership potential.

In other words, I am arguing that the difference isn't simply a coincidence. It is a product of tacit values that shape how people think about their environment and elements of organizational structure such as leadership. I am not arguing that one of these is better or worse (although I do have an opinion), but that the fact that UT Austin has never had anything other than a white male president and that UML has in recent years had both female and non-white presidents, tells us something about the context of tacit values that shape how the organizations function. What seems clear is that UML as an organization operates in a context that is more focused on questions of diversity than does UT. In fact, this is evident in the overt values of the institution as seen in UML's value statement, which I have abridged—it's much longer than UT's:

> The University of Massachusetts Lowell, as a public higher education institution of the Commonwealth, recognizes its responsibility to promote the interests and welfare of the public it serves. We are a community dedicated to learning, teaching, pursuing new knowledge through scholarly works and serving society. Each member of the community contributes to the goals of the institution through their unique and individual talents.
>
> As a community of unique individuals, we have a shared commitment to uphold core values of *respect* for all persons, *integrity* in all of our interactions and *social justice* for all. We, at UMass Lowell, strive to advance a climate whereby equity, transparency, fairness, safety and inclusion are valued so that all of its members, faculty, staff and students, can fully engage and thrive.
>
> We commit to an institutional vision and leadership that centers diversity, equity, social justice and inclusion and advocates for transparency and systemic change.

The UML values statement includes a range of values, such as diversity and social justice, that are not included in the UT statement. This does not mean that people, including leaders, at both institutions don't necessarily share these values. But public institutions create value statements that reflect the political and social climate in which they operate. Texas recently banned hiring of employees working on Diversity, Equity, and Inclusion (DEI) initiatives and banned training in DEI at public universities. In fact, diversity offices on Texas universities are illegal and UT Austin president, Jay Hartzell, fired over fifty employees who were working in areas devoted to DEI initiatives, such as the Campus Community Engagement Division, while also returning eight associate and assistant deans to faculty positions. A similar event is highly unlikely at UML, in part because the political climate of Massachusetts is quite different from that of Texas.

And this is important, because it brings us to the gist of the reason why the idea of organizational culture is so problematic. *Organizations do not exist in cultural vacuums.* In fact, decisions, structures, and values reflect the contexts in which those organizations operate and in which decisions are made. Not only are decisions different at UML and UT, the organizations themselves are different because they have been developed in larger social contexts that do not share all of the same values. At this point, you may be thinking, "right, but those are public institutions—they are government entities so they reflect state politics." This is correct, but it doesn't change anything. We can say the same about nongovernmental organizations like Ford or GM, even if they are private, because what they make is regulated by governmental organizations like NTHSA.

Tacit values influence any organization and often run so deeply that we don't even notice they are there. When I was a political science student at UML, I became fascinated with a book called *Locke, Rousseau, and the Idea of Consent: An Inquiry into the Liberal-Democratic Theory of Political Obligation* by Jules Steinberg (Steinberg, 1978). I suspect there is no other book in my library that has as many comments and underlines. A key concept in the book is *tacit consent.* The idea goes back to the writings of political theorist John Locke and works from the idea that people who enter a territory tacitly agree to obey the laws of that territory (Bennett, 1979, 227). So, if I hop on a plane today and get to Tokyo tomorrow, when I step

Chapter 3. Why Organizations Don't Have Cultures

off the plane I agree, whether I vocalize that agreement or not, to follow the laws of Japan. Every time you stop at a stop sign, you are tacitly consenting to the laws in place. You are not asked each time when you arrive at a stop sign, "do you agree to stop?" You simply consent to the laws and follow them—unless you live in Austin, Texas, where stop signs and red lights appear to be widely viewed as suggestions open to individual decision-making about consent.

For my purposes here, I'm not so interested in the concept of consent as I am the idea that one can tacitly agree to and follow a set of rules. When it comes to culture, this happens constantly. For example, I doubt you ever agreed to speak your native language. There was no informed consent form for you to sign when you were born that would somehow give you a basis for making a decision about whether to speak English as opposed to Chinese. There is no consent—it simply happened by virtue of where you happened to be born. This brings us back to the Sapir-Whorf hypothesis which we might rephrase as asking to what extent do cultural values evident in a particular social context tacitly shape how we experience, categorize, and respond to our world? In other words, what is the relationship between cultural values and the behavior of people who are in some way connected to a group expressing those values? Are people's identities profoundly shaped by culture or are they just nudged by the values that are expressed at a given time?

A good example of how differently people may think about the world as a result of the influence of cultural context can be find in the way Japanese use, or don't use, personal pronouns. If you are a native English speaker (or a speaker of many other European languages), you may be wondering how one would talk without making much use of personal pronouns. How do you identify if it was he or she who did X? Or how do we maintain gender neutrality without using something like "they" in place of pronouns like he and she? This isn't a problem in Japanese, because in regular conversation Japanese people generally don't make much use of personal pronouns when speaking. If I want to let you know I'm going to a store

The Myth of Organizational Culture

in Japanese, I will say something like, *"mise e ikimasu"* which translates into English literally as "go to store." In practice, it can mean I/you/we/they go to the store depending on context. If I am standing with my friend and I say the exact same sentence, and we both move toward the door, it is obvious that I mean "we" rather than "I." Normally, the context indicates who's acting, so it's unnecessary to state it overtly; when there's ambiguity, people may use a personal pronoun for clarification, but more likely they will use the name of the person in question to provide precision. This is quite different from English, where we normally use a personal pronoun, dropping it only in the case of giving a command: "Go to the store!" And we need the pronoun so much that we substitute "it" when no one is actually doing something. "It fell out of the tree...."

A reasonable question to ask is if this de-emphasis on personal pronouns in Japanese, as opposed to the emphasis on personal pronouns in English, deeply shapes identity. In fact, some scholars have argued that this is an expression of the collectivist Japanese culture as opposed to the individualistic American culture. I'm not particularly convinced about this binary. Americans can be highly collectivist—just go to a college football game and it's obvious. And Japanese can be very individualistic—Zen has profoundly shaped Japanese culture, but can be deeply focused on the internal, individual aspects of the person. There isn't really a binary here. Instead, we can see that ideologies in different contexts lean in a particular direction—American ideology certainly emphasizes individuality and Japanese ideology certainly emphasizes the importance of belonging (rather than collectivity) (Lebra, 1976, 1992). But there is a continuum, rather than a binary, and that continuum as it expresses in both cultures has people all along it.

Figure 2 may be helpful in understanding this. Most likely many Japanese live somewhere in the lower right quadrant while Americans live in the upper left. But there will be many who also inhabit the other quadrants on their respective sides of the Y axis. And people will move around within the quadrants. A Texan might profess

Chapter 3. Why Organizations Don't Have Cultures

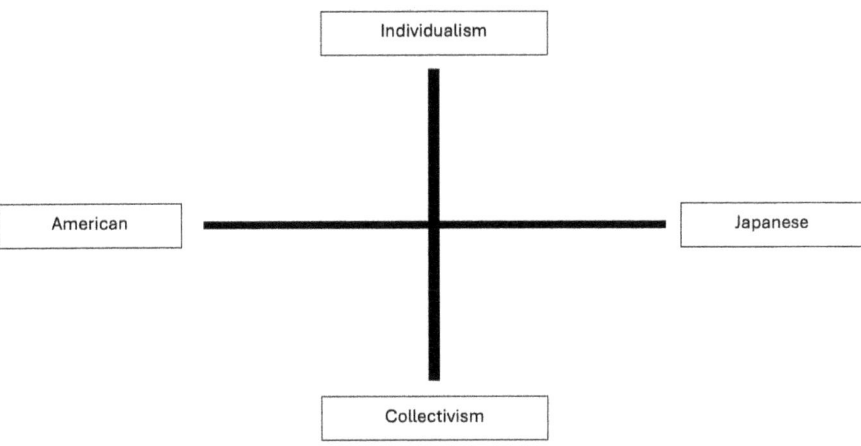

Figure 2. Culture and ideology related to individualism and collectivism.

a strong sense of rugged individualism stereotypical of American ideology, but also don burnt orange clothing and posturing, like 90,000 other people in the stadium, when participating in a University of Texas football game. Humans tend to adopt different aspects of a particular ideological framework depending on the context in which they are operating at a given time. It is strategically appropriate to conform when behaving as a fan at a football game, while a heavy dose of individualism may be appropriate when discussing the role of government in daily life. If you don't believe me, try going to a football game in Texas and remain seated during the national anthem. You will likely receive at least angry stares and more likely nasty comments. What if you aren't an American? Should you stand? Strategically, it's probably easier to conform in that situation and just stand up with everyone else, although one might decide to remain seated to make a point about American society or politics.

It's difficult to characterize either Japanese culture or American culture as being uniformly individualistic or collectivist, even if ideologies associated with these concepts are powerful in shaping behavior in each context. Ideological constructs may indicate what expected behavior is within a particular cultural context, but

The Myth of Organizational Culture

that does not necessarily mean that people are always expected to behave according to those ideologies. And, in fact, most societies have multiple ideological frameworks that contain mutually exclusive propositions. How does one reconcile the American values of individualism and free speech with values that emphasize respect for authority? This is exactly the predicament that arose during pro–Palestinian demonstrations. University leaders were faced with a question: which value system matters more? Deference to authority or free expression of political beliefs? At the MIT, Harvard, the University of Texas and many other schools the answer was clear: deference to authority is the primary value. Leaders at those schools chose to bring in the police to enforce their ideological beliefs. Other schools, like Northwestern, Brown, and Rutgers took a different approach, negotiating with students and agreeing to things like hiring more staff and instructors with knowledge of Palestine, as Rutgers did.

This brings me to the problem of thinking about organizations as having cultures. Culture and language are closely tied together and both begin shaping how we see and experience the world from birth (or perhaps even before). When our parents speak to us, we begin constructing a sense of reality that will influence everything we do in the future. This is a process, so it continually changes as we age, but there are basic parameters set deeply early in life that regulate how we think about and react to the world—and these parameters are different depending on the language framework and cultural context in which you are born. Basically, culture is a way of talking about the incredibly complex algorithms humans carry in their heads and use to interpret, manipulate, and manage their surroundings and through that create meaning. The extent to which those algorithms overlap among members of a group can be thought of as a cognitive domain and these tend to shape and limit the ways we think about the world and make assumptions about what's normal and abnormal. Language, of course, plays a big role in filtering the construction of those algorithms in individual heads, although it's not the only way we develop these—all of our senses are used to

Chapter 3. Why Organizations Don't Have Cultures

construct the reality that's experienced as a particular cultural context. Ideologies are also tied into this as frameworks for generating beliefs and ideas based on assumptions about the world.

So why don't organizations have cultures? *Because organizations are themselves expressions of cultural algorithms operating in a particular context.* Organizations built in the U.S. operate differently from those built Japan or France, because the algorithms in the heads of people in those organizations are different. People aren't born into organizations and aren't socialized from birth to think in terms of organizational membership, although group membership is certainly important. They come to organizations when they're older and have already established patterns of behavior drawn from the cultural context in which they were born and have been socialized. Organizations reflect cultural patterns associated with the contexts in which they are born—just like people. Of course, organizations are made up of individuals, and that's the reason they reflect those cultural patterns. The organizations people usually encounter first in American life are church and school. These are organizations specifically designed to shape that process of cultural learning; they operate as structures intended to inculcate people into very specific ways of seeing the world. The educational system, for example, creates individuals in the U.S. (and many other countries) who tend to see assessment of success in terms of quantities like test scores or, later, salaries. There isn't much emphasis on things like happiness or aesthetics of life in the American educational system and this is reflected in how Americans tend to see the world. Again, people can change and push back against prevailing patterns, but our early experience of organizational paradigms in places like school or church reflect broader cultural patterns in which those organizations function and, thus, shape the individuals who teach and are being taught how to be a person in that context.

Organizations do have something akin to culture (what I am calling an organizational paradigm), because there is a social environment with rules, expressed and tacit values, and power

The Myth of Organizational Culture

relationships that function in any group of humans. But this isn't a culture—culture is far more complicated. The problem with using the culture concept to think about organizations is that simply writing new value statements, doing a reorg, or having some culture training doesn't really do much because all of those things are a reflection of the larger culture in which the organization functions. They aren't a way to create culture—that job has already been done well beyond the structural boundaries of the organization that shapes everything people in the organization think and do. One way to think about this is to imagine all of the memes and pithy quotations you see on LinkedIn. A favorite of mine was one I read attributed to Bill Marklein: "Culture is how employees' hearts and stomachs feel about Monday morning on Sunday night." If I understood what this means, I'm sure I'd be envious that one could think about culture in such a simple way. But I don't really get the meme, because it so thoroughly simplifies the concept of culture as to render it meaningless. Another one posted by the same person states, "you cannot become a great leader before becoming a good human being...." I suppose, but doesn't that depend on some things like how you define a great leader and how you define a good human being? I think Adolf Hitler was quite successful at leading people, but he was among the worst examples of a human being our species has managed to produce.

Memes like these are examples of reductionism, or the practice of describing a complex phenomenon in overly simplistic ways. Sometimes this can be valuable as a means of isolating certain features of the world, but when it comes to human social organization, reductionist approaches tend to obfuscate complexity and misrepresent the way humans analyze and interpret the world. The result is that they mislead us into thinking that what we observe is much simpler than it actually is—and this is why the culture concept is so problematic when thinking about organizations. It misrepresents human social organization and behavior as being vastly less complex and easier to understand than the empirical reality before us. And

Chapter 3. Why Organizations Don't Have Cultures

ask yourself a question: Is it a good idea to make decisions based on overly simplistic and misleading understanding?

Key Takeaways

- *Individuals bring culture to their organizations.*
- *Organizations are embedded in cultural flows that shape and often restrict how they function.*
- *Thinking in terms of organizational culture confuses things, because it ignores the fact that organizations are reflections of culture rather than having cultures themselves.*
- *The organizational culture concept reduces a complex process to an overly simple property of organizations that does not reflect reality.*

Chapter 4

Organizational Ideologies and Paradigms

A few years ago, a dean in my college sent an email to department chairs. The email told everyone that we were going to form groups in which representatives from departments and programs in the College of Liberal Arts would talk about curriculum issues. The stated objective was to get departments thinking about how to improve their programs and to rethink what they were doing at the time. There was a lot of grumbling as departments set up committees to rethink the way they did things, even if they didn't think the way they did things needed to be rethought. Most would agree that there are always areas for improvement, but rethinking is a different matter—why *rethink* what is working well? A lot of people noted that this would probably end like most things do in the university—after a lot of talk and time spent, reports would be sent to upper-level "leaders" where they would enter the black hole of administration never to be seen again. And that's exactly what happened. It was a breathtaking waste of time and energy.

Most of us just responded by thinking—or saying—"that's how universities work." So, is this the organizational culture of the university? The typical definition of organizational culture would force us to answer yes. Some in organizational studies would claim it's a bad culture, maybe some would argue it's a good culture because it generates discussion. I don't know. I also don't think this aspect of how my employer operated was evidence of its culture. The University of Texas at Austin has an organizational paradigm that shapes

Chapter 4. Organizational Ideologies and Paradigms

the way things work and that paradigm is itself shaped by ideological constructs evident both within and beyond the confines of the university. One component of the paradigm, which is common among many universities, involves (endless) committee meetings that often don't really lead to any clear action. The reason universities operate this way, in part, is because the power structure of most universities is relatively flat, due to the emphasis on collective governance that has characterized higher education operations in the U.S. for over a century. Under this model deans are not bosses, nor are departmental chairs. They are administrative leaders who, normally, come out of the faculty ranks and thus remain, conceptually at least, members of the faculty. Over the past few decades, there has been a bold attack on this model coming from conservative political camps as well as from higher education administrators themselves, many of whom want to adopt a corporate hierarchical structure in which people like college deans and department chairs are, in fact, bosses. Tenure has a way of levelling the organizational playing field and creating an environment in which anyone can openly voice their opinions which means decisions need to be made collectively. This is part of the reason tenure itself is now under attack. The power associated with tenure slows things down and often leads to inefficiencies in implementing new ideas. It doesn't always work that way, because if there is buy-in to a new idea, most people will work hard to make it happen. But the wheels of higher education often move slowly—which is not necessarily a bad thing and is closely tied to two key factors.

First, because the paradigm of higher education is built around tenure and the idea of collective governance, power is distributed somewhat evenly among many, but not all, members of the faculty. But this sort of distribution of power is not particularly efficient, and this sort of structure arose because efficiency was not a core value in higher education for a long time. Rather, the primary core value has been an emphasis on discourse and debate—or the exchange of ideas. Because that is valued above efficiency, a degree of inefficiency is tolerated. There is a basic assumption in this, that intellectual exchange is more important than getting things done quickly or than economic considerations. I will leave readers to decide for themselves if this is a good prioritization of values—I think it is. The salient point here is that if you start with different assumptions about core values, you will end up with different structures in which social interactions occur. And there is not necessarily one value, such as efficiency, that should be the primary concept shaping an organizational paradigm.

This brings us to the second factor—ideology. The assumption that efficiency is of high importance or necessary in all organizational structures is based on the ideology of neoliberalism which is itself tied to ideologies associated with capitalism and liberal democracy. Before we unpack this point, it will be helpful to go into greater detail about the way in which I am using the term ideology. As Terry Eagleton notes, ideology is a word with a variety of definitions (Eagleton, 2024). Eagleton provides a list of these definitions recognizing that in some cases they are mutually exclusive. For example, one definition presents ideology as ideas used to legitimize dominant political power. This is similar to the way I defined the term in Chapter 1. But it also can be defined as ideas and thoughts motivated by social interests, or identity thinking, or action-oriented sets of beliefs, or false beliefs about the world. The list is long. Of course, if ideology is used to legitimize dominant power structures, then it can't also be a set of ideas that motivate social interests, because those who dominate are not the only ones with social interests. There is, however, one aspect that these two definitions have in common. They both conceptualize ideology in relation to power.

At this point, hopefully you are realizing that social scientists have an extremely difficult time defining key things that they study, like culture, ideology, and power. This isn't because they are dumb (well, some probably are). It's because human behavior isn't easy to characterize neatly, which means that the concepts we use inherently have limitations that force us to keep refining and rethinking how those concepts are best defined and employed to describe and analyze human behavior. This is not a weakness. It is a product of the way the world is and the fact that we cannot capture all aspects of anything with simple or even very complex definitions. It is also good science, because it recognizes the basic truth that we don't have all the answers and need to keep thinking in order to improve our understanding of a constantly changing social environment. Understanding the contingent nature of our knowledge of the world is one of the great strengths of scientific research.

Going back to ideology, Eagleton argues that dominant people, and I would argue most anyone attempting to wield power, dominant or otherwise, tend to legitimize themselves by promoting social objects—like mission and value statements—intended to unify people and create feelings of naturalness and universality about the ideas those social objects express. Humans are social animals and they tend to like things that unify them within specific social groups. This is why people want to wear college branded t-shirts or put stickers on their cars that identify them as things like a graduate of Indiana University, a veteran of the Air Force, or a fan of the Red Sox. The identification with social groups and objects that symbolize those groups generates a sense of obviousness and inevitability about the meanings associated with those social objects and allows for the easy denigration, exclusion, and obscuring of rival perspectives (Eagleton, 2024). While this process can create feelings of unity, it is also a process of legitimization often that either overtly or covertly obscures or even suppresses social conflicts or even the potential to engage in social conflict. The presentation of ideological tropes like those found in mission and values statements generates a context in which there is often an assumed—and imaginary—belief that social conflicts and conflicting belief systems are not, in fact, of consequence or even present within an organization. In other words, social objects (ideological structures) like mission statements are inherently political, meaning they involve the authoritative allocation of cultural resources like the (assumed) proper and accepted interpretation of values in a social context (Easton, 1981), and represent components

The Myth of Organizational Culture

in the exercise of power through which organizational order is maintained or, in some cases, can be challenged.

This brings us back to the issue of efficiency and how we conceptualize what it means for an organization to run well. This is an ideological question, because it depends on what is valued by a particular group and who has the power and authority to determine what should be valued. In other words, efficiency is not an objective condition that defines a good organization or a good culture—*it is a value*. To understand this, let's think about cars again, since I like cars a lot. Have you ever wondered why a Toyota Prius looks the way it does and why many other compact hybrid cars look similar? The answer is efficiency. The basic shape of the Prius came about because it generates a low drag co-efficient, which increases efficiency of airflow that improves gas mileage. It's one among many factors that allows a Prius to be so fuel efficient. It's also a factor that makes the Prius at best mundane and at worst outright ugly to look at, depending on your perspective. I have not run into many people who claim the Prius is a beautiful car. Now let's return to my father's 1968 Pontiac GTO. Unlike the Prius, it was not particularly efficient when it came to gas mileage; my father always kept a log of his mileage and as noted earlier he would get excited when he got more than ten miles per gallon on a tank. From the perspective of efficiency, as defined along Prius' emphasis on minimal usage of gasoline, our GTO was a complete disaster.

Aesthetically, however, the car is a different story. The lines are, in my view, beautiful. And it wasn't efficiency that sold the car to my father, because in 1968 Americans largely didn't care much about fuel efficiency. Gas was cheap. The prevailing values at that time emphasized other things. In the case of muscle cars, what mattered most was aesthetics and straight-line performance specs like 0–60 time. And in the case of the GTO the aesthetics weren't just about the way it looked, but the way it sounded. When looking to trade that problematic Chevy Corvair, my father and I went to the local Pontiac dealer to look at Firebirds, another lovely car. As we were

Chapter 4. Organizational Ideologies and Paradigms

talking with the salesman, workers were bringing a green GTO with a black vinyl top into the showroom. The car idled with a low rumble that caught our attention. It stood there with a low, throaty growl that sounded delicious. The GTO was more expensive than a Firebird, but we left having purchased that green GTO. The sound of that engine was bewitching and it sold the car. When it came to going from zero to sixty, the GTO was also rather efficient—we could get to sixty miles per hour very quickly due to the power transferred to the rear wheels from that huge, gas guzzling 400ci engine. That same transfer made the car a disaster to drive in the winter. If my father parked where there was ice, he would have to get someone to give him a push to get the car rolling because there was so much torque going to the rear wheels they would just spin on the ice. When it comes to the Prius and the GTO, there is no way to say which car is better. It depends on one's values. If fuel efficiency and environmental protection is valued, the Prius wins. Hands down. If aesthetics is valued, the GTO wins, although this is more subjective. If performance in a straight line is valued ... well, there isn't even much point in talking about the Prius in comparison to the GTO.

Efficiency is a value that's part of an ideological framework applied in many organizations and a value that often trumps other values such as aesthetics, open debate, or quality. But this ideological framework does not exist in a cultural vacuum. In the past, universities were not all that efficient, and they still aren't when it comes to faculty decision-making. But values in American society have changed over the past several decades and the notion of the university itself has changed from one in which it used to be seen as an intellectual or learning community to one in which it is largely seen as a business that produces research and graduates for the business world. This is tied to the growth of the broader ideology of neoliberalism, which has shifted how we think about institutions like schools and, as a result, among other things tried to pull decision-making away from academics and instead place it in the hands of full-time administrators (read business leaders). This shift in values has been

The Myth of Organizational Culture

accompanied by defunding of public universities by state governments, which has intensified the need of public universities to adopt a business model of operations simply to insure there is enough cash to run the institution. It's also tied to a changing idea about the purpose of higher education. In the neoliberal ideology, higher education is about job training. The reason one goes to college is to get a job that pays more money than one would receive without that education or degree. This is usually described as a "better" job, because the value associated with work in the neoliberal ideology is always tied to money. The things that make something good or bad are measured in terms of how much money they produce and use. Efficiency is everything in this model, because the primary value of neoliberalism reduces life to the idea that having more money is what matters most. It allows you to have more of the things you want, like a big house, fancy car, and even power. If, however, you value something else, like aesthetics or critical thinking, money is not going to be the primary measure and economic efficiency will no longer be a core value. Efficiency may not even be particularly meaningful or may be defined differently. We might think about economy of thought—as in clear thinking—rather than economic efficiency measured by costs and income. This, in fact, is how a liberal arts education has been understood in the U.S. The value structure emphasizes the production of good thinkers and good citizens, as opposed to good money-makers and consumers. We are amidst a shift in how higher education is conceptualized—determination of the values upon which it is based—that may relegate the liberal arts model to the ash heap of history.

This is not a new phenomenon. The purpose, and thus the values, associated with education in the United States have changed over the course of the country's existence. During the colonial era, colleges like Harvard (founded in 1636) were created to train clergy so that they could go out and do their religious thing among the growing population of puritans inhabiting the Commonwealth of Massachusetts. Harvard, in fact, was named for a clergyman who gave

Chapter 4. Organizational Ideologies and Paradigms

money to support the fledgling college. By the time Thomas Jefferson founded the University of Virginia in 1812, ideas about the purpose of education had changed, becoming much more closely tied to the health of America's new democracy. In a letter to L.W. Tazewell in 1805, Jefferson wrote "the people are safe depositories of their own liberty, and ... are not safe unless enlightened..." (*The Role of Education*, n.d.). Jefferson argued often that every citizen in a free society needed the information and the critical thinking skills necessary to understand their duties to others as well as to know their rights. Education, for Jefferson, wasn't about work or getting a job; it was about producing citizens who could function well in a democratic society. This makes a great deal of sense; if you are going to allow regular people to decide about how to govern, they need to have the intellectual tools to do that well. The ideological framework that Jefferson espoused was intended to generate a paradigm of higher education in the U.S. that reflected the value of citizenship and its associated rights and responsibilities, which was seen as central to maintaining a free society. This same ideological framework also has the byproduct of generating organizational paradigms in which power is diffuse and this often slows down the workings of academic organizations. Tenure is a key component of this paradigm, because it allows people to challenge each other openly, without concern about being fired. It's not, as many on the right argue, just about letting professors keep their cushy jobs. Tenure reflects values held more broadly in American (and many other) societies that value free expression of ideas. It is a part of the organizational paradigm of most universities; but it exists because it reflects and is viewed as important in maintaining larger societal or cultural values.

Culture, like language, is deeper than a paradigm. It's something we embody from the time we're born through observations of others, like our parents and teachers. It makes us unconsciously bow instead of shaking hands when meeting a new person or leads us to believe that one religion is true while others are false. It makes us think the name "John" sounds normal, but "Ryounosuke" sounds odd, or *vice*

The Myth of Organizational Culture

versa. My wife gets a kick out of the fact that people like to name their dogs "John" in Japan, but that doesn't really seem like a dog name to me. There's no right or wrong here; it's a matter of what we have learned across years of socialization, at the core of our being, to view as normal and natural. John makes a perfectly good dog name if that's what you grew up thinking is a good name for dogs. Culture *defines what is normal and natural.* Ideology takes that a step further and normalizes what is *perceived as or assumed to be a shared worldview* and, through various power structures, makes it seem as though these worldviews are uncontested and unproblematic.

The Process of Making Our World

This normalization process is so intense that a French sociologist named Pierre Bourdieu (1930–2002), developed a theory for thinking about power as it is expressed and understood in relation to culture and social change. Bourdieu approached the idea of power through a concept known as habitus, which in many ways is akin to the idea of culture but emphasizes the deep, embodied nature of our culturally shaped behaviors. Bourdieu defines habitus several times throughout his writing, but the version I find most useful is also the simplest. Habitus is the cognitive and motivating structures of a society (Bourdieu, 1977). It consists of the models our brains use to interpret the world and represent ourselves to others. We can think of it as socialized norms of behavior that shape things so deeply we rarely challenge those assumptions and ideas about the world. Habitus is created through social processes constantly influenced by individual thinking and behavior, while also limiting the scope of our thoughts and behaviors.

I remember a very clear example of this from my elementary school days. I don't remember which teacher said it, but we were taught that putting one's hands in one's pockets was not a good idea. I have no idea why, although I vaguely remember it was somehow

Chapter 4. Organizational Ideologies and Paradigms

related to posture. For a long time, I didn't put my hands in my pockets, because it seemed unnatural—something one shouldn't do. At some point, I realized, perhaps not even consciously, that this is stupid. I stopped worrying and now I put my hands in my pockets. This shows that habitus is not deterministic—our behaviors can be profoundly shaped by habitus, but we can also change what we think and do as we experience the world. I doubt in public schools there is much conversation now about putting hands in pockets. In short, habitus isn't fixed, although the patterns of thinking and behavior it generates are both enduring and can be transferred across contexts of social interaction; they also keep changing because people are constantly interpreting them and innovating or improvising. An important thing to understand about habitus is that it doesn't fit well into the long-standing debate in the West about free will as opposed to determinism. Habitus is not deterministic—it can be contested and changed. However, we also are not completely free to think and do anything. Had Newton's laws of motion never been developed, it wouldn't have mattered how smart Einstein was when he came along—he would not have been able to develop his ideas about relativity without that prior knowledge. What we know and what we do happens in a context that limits, but does not completely restrict, what we can do and what we can think. It creates a form or structure, but that structure (just like in the arts) is something that can be challenged and can lead to novel observations and ideas, like Einstein's theory of relativity.

Habitus involves a feedback loop in which there is a constant interplay between free will and deterministic (power) structures in society that draws on past events and experiences which continue to shape how we interpret and construct current and future practices (Bourdieu 1984:170). This process does not involve any necessary attempt to identify coherency in practice (ideologies need not be consistent nor logical) nor does it demand conscious awareness of what is going on. All of this happens within what Bourdieu identifies as "fields," which are the social and institutional frameworks within which people constantly express their ideas and identities and through which those ideas and identities are reproduced. Who you are is a product of this ongoing process. Your identity is generated in relation to the social context in which you exist, but that social context is also changing as a result of the simple fact that you live in it, interpret it, and act on the basis of what you come to believe about it. That context, what Bourdieu refers to as a field, can be understood as a multidimensional network of human relationships through which who and what we are is constantly being defined and redefined, which, in turn, defines and redefines the network itself. These networks are found in various organizational contexts, such as those connected to religious, educational, business, or governmental aspects of society. These networks, which are essentially what I am calling organizational paradigms, are the circuit boards through which humans exercise and exchange power in social interactions.

Individual bodies (and I state bodies here because this happens at the physical level), interpret their world and through those interpretations generate practices—the things they do. Those practices influence ideas, values, and beliefs which, in turn, generate a social milieu that seems unquestionably natural and normal. This is habitus. Habitus, of course, shapes how we function. It shapes how we interpret ourselves and how we interpret our surroundings. In many ways, it is imprinted on us physically. The way we gesture (do we use our hands when we talk or do we bow a lot?), the clothes we select, even the quality and timbre of our voices are products of habitus. If you listen to how people talk in different parts of a society, you will notice not only that they have different accents or dialects, but their voices can sound quite different, but they sound similar to others who have grown up in the same context. We learn to use our voices through mimesis, or the action of observing and copying what those around us do and embodying what we experience (Taussig, 2018). Culture provides us with a framework for deciding what does and does not sound good in terms of how we speak. You may find

Chapter 4. Organizational Ideologies and Paradigms

yourself disliking the way people with a particular accent speak your language and are probably more comfortable with those who sound more like you. Most of us do this. I'm far more comfortable around people who speak with a Boston accent than with any form of Texas accent.

Figure 3 will help to make this process clearer. Our bodies/minds experience social (and environmental) context, which is what we are calling habitus. We constantly interpret our experiences, and this process generates ideas, values, and beliefs about that context, which we continually interpret. We can call this combination of experience and interpretation *ideology*. Ideology, in turn,

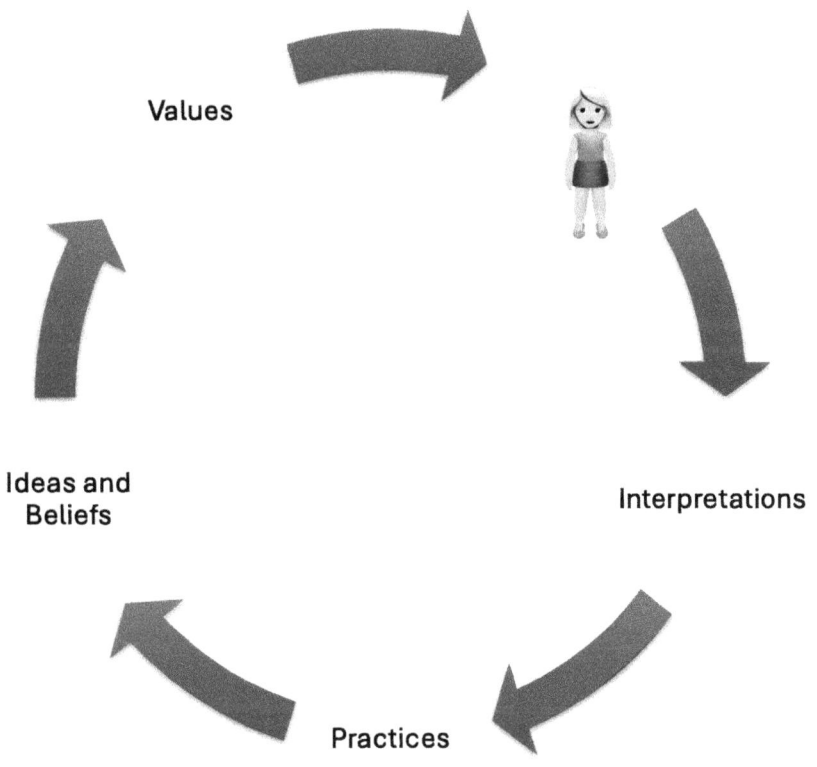

Figure 3. Process of identity formation in relation to habitus.

shapes the things we do—the practices we carry out in the world and those practices inform habitus, which continues to shape our bodies/minds. This is an ongoing cycle in which all of us are embedded. But it's essential to recognize that we have agency. We can influence the cycle through our actions, thus the cycle is not *deterministic* in terms of our identities, but instead is *influential*. It shapes us, but we shape it back. One point is essential to understand—there is no right or wrong here. The process happens regardless of the values associated with it. And the process occurs at all levels of human experience, from the broad cultural context in which we live to the more narrow organizational paradigms in which we encounter and interact with specific groups of individuals.

When I was in graduate school, my wife (who was also in graduate school) introduced me to the work of a brilliant linguist named William Labov who is largely attributed with founding the field of sociolinguistics. Labov visited the University of Pittsburgh while we were graduate students there and we managed to get into his very packed talk—which was disappointingly dry. But his ideas, as well as his research methods, are brilliant. Lobov was interested in how we use language from a cultural perspective and how that intersects with the ways in which we represent ourselves—our identities—to others. He did a study of people living on Martha's Vineyard and noticed something interesting about how they use dialects (Labov, 2014). I'm over-simplifying here, but basically those people who were highly invested in the local community tended to retain stronger local dialects while those who were interested in moving away, such as to Boston, tended to adopt a more generalized Boston accent. He also found that people wanting to move to the Vineyard would in some cases affect a form of the local accent. There is a lot more going on in his research, but the basic point was that people shift the ways they use language, including their accents, strategically to achieve desired goals. Of course, this also can influence the local dialect itself. If many people on Martha's Vineyard who work at shops adjust their dialect to make it easier to communicate

Chapter 4. Organizational Ideologies and Paradigms

with tourists from places like Boston and New York, the local dialect itself will begin to change over time. Dialect and accent are not static conditions in which we learn and produce language—they are processes.

This is an excellent example of how habitus works. People, with either overt or unconscious intentions, adjust their behavior and that behavior changes the context or habitus. I noticed this in myself after I moved to Texas. Perhaps to try to fit in a bit, I started to use y'all. But it felt odd to me and I soon stopped. I also noticed over time that some aspects of my Boston accent became more pronounced the longer I lived in Texas. This is unlikely a coincidence; the longer I lived in Texas, the more I came to deeply dislike it. There is good reason to think that subconsciously I adopted more typical Boston speech patterns as a way of making it clear to others that I was an outsider—not a Texan. Both of my children use y'all naturally—but it still sounds weird to me when they do. There is no right or wrong here. The salient point is that we manipulate our identities as a way of managing the social contexts in which we function. This also has an influence on any context we inhabit. The first time students told me I had a northern accent, I was surprised. I had never thought of myself as having a northern accent, but to them it was very clear. And in a small way, simply hearing that accent—and interpreting me and how I see the world as a result of what I said in class with that accent—changed the local context, because it changed the people in my class. This process has much in common with Darwinian evolution, in which minuscule influences continually change the context in which organisms are functioning and dealing with their surroundings.

The process of acquiring culture, habitus, or whatever we want to call it, generates a set of cognitive and motivating structures—or algorithms—in our heads that not only shape behavior, but provide a scaffold for constructing reality itself and through that applying meaning to our experiences. These become so normalized that we often don't even question the idea that how we see the world is natural and normal for everyone. This isn't quite the same as what's going on in organizations. In organizations, we create systems—organizational structures, policies and procedures, ideologies, etc.—that shape what we can and cannot do. We don't really have to buy into these rules and structures in order to function successfully. We just have to be willing to follow the rules. This is different from culture, because we don't necessarily accept those rules and structures as natural and normal. Instead, we often view them as the organization's way of doing things and consciously align our ideas and attitudes to fit. This is usually necessary if we want to keep our job. This behavior is more like what happens when you live in a cultural context that is not native for you. If you don't learn the language when you move long-term to a new cultural context, you will struggle to do things and in some places you may even be ostracized. You will likely feel like an outsider and in many cases the presence of your accent while using the local language will forever remind you that you are, in fact, an outsider, even if people are relatively welcoming. Much of this depends on how one perceives of their own needs. If you move to a new place and intend to be there permanently, there's a good chance you will adjust your behaviors and attitudes to align with prevailing ideas about what is normal and natural. If you think it's temporary, you may not do so. Human identity is fluid and we routinely adjust it in subtle or even major ways to allow us to function well in social contexts. But there are also limits on what we will do, depending on the extent to which we value belongingness within a given social context.

All of this, of course, happens within organizations, but that is because organizations are embedded in larger cultural and social contexts that consist of individual humans who behave like individual humans. Like the individuals who form it, an organization is an expression of habitus while also influencing it. One of the main problems with thinking of organizations as if they have their own cultures is that this creates a misleading sense that there are social walls around the organization that somehow isolate it from the larger

Chapter 4. Organizational Ideologies and Paradigms

context in which it operates. This is one of the main reasons we need to move away from the organizational culture concept. Organizations are not isolated entities with their own cultures; they are cultural *products*. Even while creating localized ways of doing things, those ways also reflect larger cultural and ideological trends and patterns. Organizations do, however, have structures, or organizational paradigms, through which practice is circumscribed. Things like mission statements, org charts, and compensation packages are elements of organizational paradigms. Minor changes in these don't have much influence on the system as a whole, major changes—such as a large reorg or the firing of a CEO—will generate ripples and waves that run through the entire organization.

These organizational paradigms exist inside and are shaped by cultural contexts—the same cultural contexts in which the individuals who make up the local organizational paradigm are embedded. Therefore, each paradigm reflects assumptions commonly held by people in the cultural context. If leaders of an organization attempt to develop a paradigm far outside of cultural norms—and that may be quite difficult to even imagine doing—there is a good chance that the organization will fail. So, when the CEO of company X states that she wants to make "responsibility" a key value of the company and uses that to create a corporate "culture," she is actually drawing on a concept that has been constructed in her head as she's grown and changed over her life course. She's *applying* a value pulled from the cultural context in which her company operates, or in which she happened to grow up, and making it an overt, stated element in the ideology that defines the organizational paradigm and will hopefully guide behavior. But no matter how much said CEO wants to "create" an organizational culture around the value of responsibility, there is no guarantee everyone in the organization will interpret the meaning of responsibility in the same way. In fact, they will bring their own values to the table as they interpret the ideological concepts handed down from those in power.

Key Takeaways

- *Cultural contexts are active, not static.*
- *Humans have agency and cultural contexts are constantly changing, as are organizational paradigms, in relation to individual and collective behaviors.*
- *Assumptions about what is natural and normal are not objective, they are subjective products of the cultural context in which we are socialized.*

Chapter 5

Power as Productive Force

When the dean sent out that email about rethinking everything we do, there were a few ways department leaders could react. They could assemble the faculty, discuss the email, and develop a plan to carry out the expectations of the dean. They could largely ignore the email and go about business as usual, knowing that the entire exercise was never going to amount to any significant change. Just get someone in the department to do a "study" and write a BS report to be submitted to the dean. Make sure to include some "metrics," even if they are meaningless. It will all be forgotten anyway. Another option would be to resist the requirement and email the dean back saying that it was hard to see how this would be beneficial and that, in fact, it was a waste of time. Because of tenure, a department chair wouldn't be fired for not doing anything or even for overtly resisting. But they would get grief and might have problems successfully negotiating with the dean in the future when they wanted something like a new faculty hire or more money for graduate students.

Deans have power. They can force faculty to do things—to a point. But faculty have power, too, because many of them have tenure. If the dean of my college calls me tomorrow and says, "Jack, I'd like you to work on this project for the College." I can just say, "no" and that's the end of it. There really isn't much she can do to force me to take on the project. Of course, that's not really the end of it, because if I refuse, the next time I ask the dean for something, I'll get the same answer I gave her—No. Both the dean and I have access to social and symbolic capital, which gives us some degree of power over both what we choose to do and what we can make others do.

The Myth of Organizational Culture

In the case of the dean, she has more capital than I, because she can inhibit my ability to teach classes I want to teach or to do research I want to do. That ability is limited, but it's there. In fact, many years ago, a different dean came up with a policy to basically punish faculty who were not productive researchers. The punishment was to increase their teaching load from two courses per semester to three. This meant that tenured professors, although they had sufficient capital to keep their jobs regardless of their productivity, also were pushed to focus more on research and less on teaching—unless they were comfortable with teaching three courses per semester. The dean couldn't outright fire people for being comparatively unproductive researchers, but he could influence their working lives. The presence of tenure formed a well of social capital professors could use to keep their jobs, even if they were not particularly productive. But the nature of their jobs changed as a result of the power held by the dean. And because prestige as a faculty member at a research university is closely tied to research production and visibility, being given the teaching punishment has the potential to reduce one's status. There was a formal component to this, because lack of productivity in research normally prevents one from being promoted from associate to full professor. Note, however, that if Professor X loves teaching and doesn't care much about research, this isn't a punishment. This was recognized and administrators changed the rules to try to put more pressure on faculty to be productive researchers by creating a time-limit on how long they could stay in the rank of associate professor. But, again, there were limits because that pressure only worked for unproductive associate professors. For someone who had attained the rank of full professor, it didn't mean anything.

All human interactions involve power. Please stop reading for a moment and think about that statement. It is a vast generalization. As an anthropologist, I'm not terribly inclined to like large generalizations. But I think this one is right. *All human interactions involve power.* See if you can think of an example where this isn't true. If

Chapter 5. Power as Productive Force

you're trying to convince someone to buy a product, or to go on a date with you, you are creating a power relationship in which ideas and behaviors are exchanged and interpreted to accomplish a particular goal. This isn't simply a matter of vertical power relationships in which people above wield power over those below. Horizontal relationships also involve the expression of power both in the attempt to convince others that one's ideas make sense and in the reaction to those ideas, positive or negative. If I go to McDonald's and order a Big Mac meal and the cashier asks, "do you want that large sized?" it's a power relationship. She is, perhaps quite subtly, trying to get me to spend more money. Neither she nor I may even be aware that there is a subtle power exchange going on, but it's there. If you tell your spouse, "I love you" it might seem like there is no power relationship. But the fact is, you are likely expecting a similar response—the statement is not only a means to convey emotional information, it's also a means to elicit emotional information. How do you feel if your spouse simply doesn't respond?

In making this large claim, I'm also pushing myself into a corner, because I need to clearly indicate what I mean by the word power. Like the word culture, power is constantly employed in American society, but its meanings can be both diverse and fuzzy. Think of the different idioms in which the term is used: money is power, power breakfast, power tie, knowledge is power, be on a power trip, more power to you, power of good, power of evil, lust for power, flower power, Black power, power nap, grey power. I think you get the point. The term is used frequently but not in a consistent way. A power tie is obviously different from a power nap, and which is it, money or knowledge, that equals power? Of course, it gets even messier if we think about things like electrical power or horsepower. Americans use the term power frequently, and unfortunately the word "power" has come to carry somewhat negative connotations in American society. We often think of power as something exerted over us or as an instrument of coercion, rather than a tool that can be used to accomplish individual and collective goals or a fundamental component of human relationships. You've probably already guessed where I'm going—we need to define what we mean by power.

One thing is clear, when it comes to power some people have more access to it than others. Access to power is not something distributed equally across individual humans nor across different groups. When Europeans invaded North America, there was an inherent differential in power between the invaders and the indigenous peoples. Part of this was technological—Europeans had things like guns. Part of it was also a matter of circumstance. Europeans brought with them various infectious diseases usually in a dormant state, like smallpox and cholera, for which people living in North America had little immunity. This caused outbreaks of disease that unintentionally killed millions over time, although there were also intentional attempts to infect indigenous people such as the presenting of smallpox infected blankets at Fort Pitt in Pennsylvania (Koch, Brierley, Maslin, & Lewis, 2019). Even without specific intent, however, the arrival of Europeans in North American was part of a very large expression of power associated with colonization and dominance over indigenous peoples that at times involved attempts at influence (such as through trade) and at other times involved the direct use of force through warfare.

In 1957, political scientist Robert Dahl published an important article in which he argued that power involves interpersonal relations and carries symbolic content. He defines power in a rather direct way: "A has power over B to the extent that he can get B to do something that B would not otherwise do" (Dahl, 1957, 203). This is a helpful definition, because it encourages us to think not only about what power is, but how it works. There are several different ways for A to get B to do something B wouldn't otherwise do. For example, during the demonstrations at the University of Texas about the Israeli/Palestinian war in 2024, the entire university population received an email from the chief of the campus police department in which he "commanded" everyone to immediately leave the area in which demonstrators had set up tents. It was an odd email, since

Chapter 5. Power as Productive Force

the majority of us weren't even on campus. But it showed something about power—the police chief was convinced that he had sufficient power and the associated legitimate authority, not to ask, but to *command* that people leave. The ability to wield power can be circumscribed by the extent to which others buy-in to the idea that one has a legitimate right—the authority—to do so. Of course, the students ignored him and eventually the police moved in, forcibly (and violently) removing a group of peaceful demonstrators.

Interestingly, this use of power points to weaknesses related to the authority of decision-makers, because the fact that university leadership felt they needed to resort to coercion is an indication that there are problems with the perceived legitimacy of their leadership. As Leslie Green notes, coercion threats and coercive acts are intended to reinforce authority "when the political order fails in its primary normative technique of authoritative guidance" (Green, 1988, 75). In other words, organizations resort to coercion when there is a perceived threat to their legitimate authority to exercise power—to make others do what those in positions of power want. This is, in fact, why many university leaders cracked down on the demonstrations. The demonstrators' unwillingness to obey commands was a challenge to the authority of leadership, thus it needed to be squelched by the use of coercive power not only to stop the demonstrations but to demonstrate the fact that leadership had the power to control the demonstrators regardless of circumstances of their behavior or the content of their message. Ironically, however, that same use of coercive power is an indicator that those in power have problems related to the legitimacy of their authority to wield power, because if people see those in authority as having a legitimate well of authority, they will usually follow; but if they are unconvinced about that legitimacy, they will hold off on following which, then, often results in leaders using force to get what they want. This can happen in various ways, such as active resistance like peaceful or violent protests, passive resistance (such as a sit-in), or other types of actions like writing op ed pieces that challenge the actions and authority of those making decisions. Resort to coercion by those in positions of authority is usually a sign that leadership has significant issues with perceptions of its legitimate right to wield power. And those issues can undermine the ability of leaders to act if things begin to spin out of control. It is often when leaders feel that potential arising, and recognize the presence of overt challenges to their legitimacy as leaders, that they resort to coercive behavior.

This example leads one to think about complexities in types of power and how they relate to authority. Campus leaders at many institutions initially asked people to leave or tried to convince the demonstrators that it would be best for themselves to vacate the campus. Some university leaders who did this agreed in return to set up forums to discuss and debate issues such as divestment of university investments in Israel. This form of power is what we can call *reward power*, which depends on the ability of those wielding power to confer some sort of benefit on those attempting to be influenced. In this case, A makes B do something B wouldn't otherwise do by offering B a reward for doing it. The reason power is important here is because A can't offer anything if A lacks the power and resources to do so. If I, as a tenured professor, were to walk out onto the lawn and offer to the students that my university will discuss divestment, it would be silly because I lack the resources—the social and symbolic capital—to make the offer. I don't have the authority to do so, nor do I have the resources to set up any sort of forum for public discussion of the problem. In short, I have no power related to this. The president of the university, however, has both the power and authority to make such an offer, although there are limits because the president's power and authority are circumscribed by a larger political context in which any public university operates and may have limitations produced by the influence of wealthy donors or politicians. Indeed, the political leanings of any government will have a direct influence over the actions of leadership at public universities. This does not mean all university leaders will necessarily follow expectations set forth by government leaders, but those same members of

Chapter 5. Power as Productive Force

the government have a significant club they can use to get what they want—money. Threats to reduce funding to a public university are likely to shape how leaders of that university behave.

As noted earlier, when the president ordered the demonstrators removed, he also granted the police chief the authority necessary to command that people leave. The ability to do this is what we call *positional power*, or the legitimate right to delegate authority to the holder of a position, such as chief of police, who then can use that authority to influence or coerce B to do something B wouldn't otherwise do. In this case, the command emailed to the university community was an attempt to, not so subtly, influence the demonstrators to leave. The use of the word *command* itself implied that if they failed to comply, something more was going to happen. In fact, that something more turned out to be the use of force, or *coercive power*, to physically remove the demonstrators from campus against their will. Use of coercive power, in which the target is made to do something directly against their will, is often the last resort when less overt attempts to exert authority over others have failed.

In recent years, philosophers, sociologists, and anthropologists, among others, have spent a great deal of ink thinking about power. They've asked questions like: How is power related to influence and authority? Does power always involve coercion? And, what is power in the first place? Of course, academics debate this stuff endlessly, but some good ideas about power have come out of the debate. From my standpoint, these three observations are important about power:

1. Power is found in relationships between and among people. People have access to it in variable ways that allow them to manipulate the actions and ideas of others. In other words, they have access to capital—both symbolic and social—that gives them the ability to manipulate how other people respond to varied situations. In some cases, things like the title they hold gives them an automatic well of capital that

they can access to get people to do what they want. Police officers are an example of this. So are college professors.

2. Power doesn't just limit what people can do, it also can be productive in allowing them to accomplish things, even if they're in a weaker position. People who are disenfranchised from decision-making processes can still exert power through actions that affect those in positions of power, such as slowing down work or calling in sick. There is risk involved with this, of course, but it is still a way that power can be productively exercised by those who have limited access to power wells.

3. Power permeates our society and *all* social interactions. Again, *all human interactions involve the use of power in some way.*

Number three is of particular importance here, because it draws from the notion that power is fundamental to how humans deal with each other. This is the idea presented by French sociologist Michel Foucault, who developed a theory that power is not wielded by individuals or groups but is instead dispersed throughout society. "Power is everywhere" and is intertwined with and constituted through knowledge (Foucault, 1998, 63). In other words, Foucault dis-individualizes power, creating a sense in which it becomes a property of social interactions, rather than something individuals possess. "Power has its principle not so much in a person as in a certain concerted distribution of bodies, surfaces, lights, gazes; in an arrangement whose internal mechanisms produce the relation in which individuals are caught up" (Foucault, 1991, 202).

Something as simple as a smile across a room may have the power to influence the behavior of the person looking that direction. Many years ago, I was at a party and was doing what I usually do at parties—hiding in the corner. I generally hate parties where I know few people, so I tend to try to keep to myself and leave as quickly

Chapter 5. Power as Productive Force

as possible. A couple across the room noticed that I was alone and, apparently in their view, lonely (I wasn't lonely). They immediately started across the room to rescue me from my solitude. As the husband marched toward me with his hand out ready to shake mine, my only thought was: "How do I get out of here? Is there an open window I can jump through?" Power was employed in this case. The frightening couple were able to make me do something I had not planned on doing—look for a way out of a situation I knew I would dislike—simply by behaving in a way they thought was friendly. I doubt it ever even occurred to them that there was a power exchange unfolding as a result of their actions. Of course, my actions also involved power. When I saw them coming, I turned to look at some pictures on the wall as a way to say, "please stop." I was sending a signal that I didn't want to talk with them—it was an attempt to get them to stop doing something they wanted to do. My signal failed to get through.

In the modern world, power is often exercised through organizational or institutional structures via *discipline*, which is a modality for the exercise of power involving social instruments, motivational techniques, procedures, mission statements, etc., through which people are manipulated. Power involves actions and reactions performed in social contexts that may, but do not necessarily, involve violence and force. Essential to the use of power, however, is knowledge, which is why surveillance has become such an important part of how organizations work. Knowledge makes it easier to manipulate social contexts and, thus, to use power effectively. If you understand what your customers want, you are far more likely to have success in convincing them to buy what you are selling. If you understand what your workers are doing with their time, you are more likely to be able to make sure they are doing what you want.

I don't entirely agree with Foucault's approach to power—I think power not only permeates social contexts like organizations, but also can be a property associated with individuals and groups. One the one hand, power permeates social contexts, but it's like electricity on a circuit board. Electricity (power) moves around the circuit board and is employed in various ways by the components of the device. People are basically like capacitors, nodes in the electrical network, that store power (electrical charge on the circuit board) and release it when needed. Everyone has some access to power because all social interactions involve power relations. I suspect it would be possible to push this analogy further, but I don't want to overdo the metaphor. Humans, of course, are not capacitors, because they have the ability to make complex decisions about how and when to use the power to which they have access. The simple point I want to emphasize is that there is a similarity in how a circuit board works with the way human social interactions function as power relationships, because like electrostatic charge on a circuit board, power circulates throughout the social context and, like capacitors, individual humans store that power and use it when needed.

We can see this by drawing on two other useful concepts that have been central in social science theorizing over the past fifty years, social capital and symbolic capital, both of which were important components of Bourdieu's theoretical work. I've used the terms social and symbolic capital several times throughout this book and now it's time to be clear about what I mean by this. Social and symbolic capital refer to the social "stuff" people possess, acquire, and accumulate and which becomes a resource upon which they can draw to get other people to do something or to accomplish those things they, themselves, wish to do or to have done. A college degree contains both social and symbolic capital for the holder. *Social capital* comes from having accomplished the process of getting a degree. This form of capital is acquired as a result of having succeeded in getting admitted to and then graduating from a college along with the interactions one has with others throughout that process. Some people have access to the social capital associated with being a college graduate and others don't, and that access may be related to a variety of factors such as intellectual ability, work ethic, socio-economic status, race, gender, and so on. The depths of the well of capital also varies by individual. The student who never visits faculty during office

Chapter 5. Power as Productive Force

hours is going to have a more difficult time drawing on social capital in the form of recommendations as compared to the student who gets to know their professors well. You can spend social capital, and usually do so when doing things like applying for jobs. One way of spending it is by using the connections one gains through things like alumni networks to get access to internship, employment, or graduate school opportunities. This is something you can tap out—make too many requests of alumni for help in finding a job, or behave in ways alumni and others find inappropriate, and the door may close on access to that resource. Ask for too many letters of recommendation from a professor and they might tell you that they can't write any more (I've had this happen). Although simply completing a college degree generates some social capital, the overall social value of a degree is more complex, because you can spend down that capital over time.

Being in possession of a college degree also brings with it *symbolic capital*. You are looked at differently by many in society as a result of having a degree. A college degree brings a level of symbolic capital simply by virtue of having graduated—it doesn't matter what your GPA was. A strong GPA can add social capital (and some symbolic capital) to that degree, but the fact of having the degree confers capital in symbolic form. Higher degrees bring additional symbolic capital, many people view lawyers and doctors as inherently capable and intelligent, but there are incompetent doctors and lawyers out there who simply were good at school. Having obtained an advanced degree, they carry with them inherent capital that can also be used, but you don't really ever exhaust it. I'm a retired college professor and being a professor is something that's part of my identity and that I can make use of—but it won't ever go away. This is what symbolic capital is about. It comes with things like the title/occupation of lawyer, professor, or doctor, but it is not tied to factors such as competence or work ethic. It doesn't matter much if I was good or bad at being a college professor—I retain the title and, in fact, have a special title, emeritus professor, that indicates I'm retired but still a professor and, therefore, still in possession of symbolic capital associated with that social position.

Symbolic capital also varies in relation to where one gets a degree. Imagine identical twins who attended college at the same time, majored in the same subject, took exactly the same courses, all of their professors had the same level of publications and quality of teaching, and the twins got exactly the same grades and, thus, GPAs over four years. The *only* difference between them is that Twin A went to Yale, while Twin B went to the University of Massachusetts Lowell (UML). If both twins apply for the same job, which one is likely to get an offer? There's a good chance the one who went to Yale will. I graduated from both institutions and would argue that the quality of education I received at UML was significantly better than what I received at Yale, which was still very good. The professors were far more engaged in the education of students and my classes were wonderful contexts to develop strong critical thinking skills. I owe my career as a scholar to the professors in political science and history at UML. Interestingly, unlike the faculty at Yale, few of my professors at UML had PhDs, instead only having MA degrees. They had gone into college teaching during the 1960s when the south campus of UML was called Lowell State College and a PhD was not considered necessary. Those same professors would have been unemployable at Yale (as they would be today at UML) and probably would have been at least mildly looked down upon at scholarly conferences. In the academic world, a PhD brings symbolic capital that an MA degree lacks. The important point here about symbolic capital is that their status as professors was not particularly related to their abilities as teachers. Without a PhD, they simply did not have the symbolic capital to become college professors in the modern academic environment, even if they did in the 1960s at a state teacher's college.

So why would the Yale twin get the job? The answer is that the Yale degree carries with it greater symbolic capital than the UML degree. This factor's influence is deeper than simply having obtained a Yale or a UML degree. The identity of Yale twin is different from

Chapter 5. Power as Productive Force

that of UML twin, despite everything else about them and their educations being identical. Yale brings with it symbolic capital in the form of being a prestigious Ivy League school, and that prestige becomes part of Yale twin's identity. It is embodied as part of who Yale twin is as a person. Yale twin can use this form of capital, but UML twin has absolutely no access to that capital. Use of this symbolic capital may involve something as simple as putting the name of the institution on one's resume.

When I was in college, I worked at a bank. I remember very well there was a young guy—we'll call him Fred—who had rapidly risen in the bank, always wore nicely starched white shirts, suspenders, and conservative ties, and was talked about in terms of being smart, hard-working, and competent. Everyone assumed he had a bright future ahead of him. And then one day, he was gone. Fred had been fired in part because it turned out that he didn't have the symbolic capital everyone believed he possessed. He had indicated on his resume that he was an MIT graduate, but somehow it came out that he lied about that. Obviously, he was fired because he lied. But there was more to it. His lie changed his identity from one in which he held the symbolic capital associated with being an MIT graduate, to one in which not only did he lack that symbolic capital but he acquired new social capital that associated him with dishonesty. Funny thing is that I doubt he suddenly ceased being smart, hard-working, and competent. Okay, I admit we have good reason to doubt the "smart" part. But had his lie never been discovered, he likely would have continued to prosper because he possessed a combination of acquired social capital related to his behavior as a banker and symbolic capital related to the prestige value of his perceived MIT degree. And what would have happened if his lie was a bit different? Suppose he indicated that he went to Middle Tennessee State University but, in fact, went to Kent State University? Would he have been fired? I'm not sure, because the well of symbolic capital associated with these two schools isn't all that different from each other. I can imagine that he might have been reprimanded, but maybe not fired. And, oddly enough, the locus of his degree and lack of an MIT degree in no way changes his abilities as a banker or his dedication to hard work. If it did, he would have been let go earlier simply on the basis of poor performance.

Returning to our twins, we should not assume that UML twin has no symbolic capital. UML is a fine university and some of its programs are top-notch, such as engineering. If he had an engineering degree, he would most certainly have a fair amount of symbolic capital as a result of having graduated from UML. But our twins have access to different resources and different wells of symbolic capital that shape their ascribed identities (meaning the identities others attribute to them) and, through that, influence the flow of their careers and lives. This is why I don't think power is entirely dis-individualized. Because Yale twin has a resource—a form of capital—that UML twin lacks, Yale twin has the power to spend that resource in ways that are not accessible to UML twin. UML twin will probably also get a good job and over time, if they perform well, they will gain social capital that can be spent to get new jobs, raises, promotions, etc. UML twin may, in fact, have a more successful career than Yale twin, depending on how one measures that. But no matter what UML twin does, they will never have the symbolic capital Yale twin possess in relation to their degree, even if other forms of capital over time become more important in UML twin's life. Symbolic capital is a permanent (assuming it isn't the product of a lie, such as falsely claiming to be an MIT graduate) part of one's identity that other people interpret.

It's important to recognize that the boundaries between social and symbolic capital can be quite fuzzy. Think about the power of the president of the United States. Much of presidential power is invested in the office, not the person. Thus, when the person leaves office, they no longer have full access to that power because they no longer have access to the symbolic capital associated with the office itself. The power and authority to launch a nuclear strike is not something an individual maintains after leaving office. But simply by virtue

Chapter 5. Power as Productive Force

of having been president, they have accumulated social and symbolic capital which gives them the power to do many things after leaving office, such as writing best-selling books, that would be ignored if they had not been president. It's helpful to parse symbolic and social capital to understand how they work, but it's important to keep in mind that they are often deeply intertwined. Being president is achieved through an election, which one wins through effort (among the use of other things like money). This means it brings with it social capital. Being King is not achieved; it's a matter birth, which means it carries symbolic capital. But being president carries with it a degree of symbolic capital that continues after leaving office—one never loses the title of president. And one can accrue social capital as King based upon the quality of one's leadership, just as one can lose social capital as a result of bad behavior. The British monarchy has struggled with this in relation to the behavior of some of its members, while the Japanese Monarchy has largely lacked scandals and, thus, tends to be highly respected by the Japanese people. Social and symbolic capital are intertwined and are not easy to neatly disentangle.

POWER AND ORGANIZATIONAL DYNAMICS

I want to reiterate a key point of this chapter: *all social interactions involve power relationships*. This means that power operates at the micro level of social relations within and among all levels of organizations, not just as a property of macro-level decision-making from the top. Power is everywhere and humans exercise power in *strategic* ways to achieve personal and collective goals. Let's return to the museum example I discussed earlier in the book. One of the problems with the mission and value statements of the museum was that academic leadership did not interpret things in the same way those working with the public and taking care of the facility did. Imagine for a moment that some members of the janitorial staff, frustrated with the stratified social structure of the organization, decide to be

The Myth of Organizational Culture

a bit less careful in their work. Bathrooms don't get cleaned quite as well, maybe doors that should be locked aren't. It could be anything. Leadership will likely look at this as sloppy work, but if there is intent aimed at some form of organizational change, then it is clearly an attempt to exercise power. And even if there isn't specific intent, it still involves power relationships, because there will be some exercise of power to rectify the situation and potentially some resistance to that attempt. Even something as simple as calling in sick can be a conscious, or even unconscious, attempt to draw on limited access to power in order to generate some sort of personal or collective change within any organization.

While some forms of power involve obedience to law or rule makers, the flow of organizational power influences us in subtle ways. The decision to have t-shirts made for employees involves using organizational power to generate a sense of collectivity and common identity. Of course, as I have tried to make clear throughout this book, individuals do not necessarily respond to those efforts in the same or in expected ways. When I was given a burnt orange t-shirt with the College of Liberal Arts logo on it, my first thought was, "why are you wasting money on this? Use that money for faculty pay or to support student scholarships." I never wore it, of course. Vocalizing that sentiment also involves power because it would represent an attempt to push back against the prevailing flow of power and redirect it in a way that I found appropriate. That same vocalization has the potential to generate a negative response from those responsible for the t-shirt promotion (it did, when I voiced my opinion).

The flow of power in an organization is the lifeblood or the organizational paradigm that shapes things like mission and value statements. It permeates all aspects of the organization and, thus, is the most important building block in how an organizational paradigm is constructed and experienced. This is why organizational cultures—which as I've been arguing I think are much better understood as organizational paradigms—are not about things like a meme I mentioned earlier from LinkedIn claiming that organizational culture is

Chapter 5. Power as Productive Force

about how people feel about work on Sunday evening. Memes like that significantly underestimate the complexity of any organizational paradigm. An organizational paradigm is about how power relationships are exercised and experienced in the ongoing process that is any organization. It is about how people perceive of the ways in which power is deployed and how it affects them, as well as perceptions about their own access to power. Fundamentally, organizational paradigms are about the interplay of social and symbolic capital as they are expressed through human agency, which itself is expressed through the action of engaging and manipulating power structures and the people who inhabit those power structures to achieve desired ends.

Power is also closely related to knowledge and knowledge production. Mechanisms of power produce different ways of knowing and different types of knowledge that people use to organize their activities and give meaning to existence. The way of knowing what it means to work at the museum I've used as an example here is different among those on the upper floors (the academic leaders) and those on the lower floors (the people who face the public on a daily basis and take care of the facility). This is because the experience of being in those roles and inhabiting specific positions on the social hierarchy of the museum varies. Power exists inherently in this network of individuals, behaviors, and ideas that forms what we refer to as an organization. It flows through the organization and is tapped in various ways by the people who work there. It can be tapped in ways that either negatively or positively influence the paradigm that structures the organization and shapes the experience of people at all levels. If we think of the organization as a circuit board, the organizational paradigm is the layout of that circuit board. The individuals who are part of the organization are the capacitors, transistors, resistors, etc., through which power flows and that make use of that power in various ways to accomplish particular organizational and personal goals.

This brings me to a final point of this chapter. Knowledge isn't power. I know, everyone always says that knowledge is power. But it's not. Knowledge deeply influences the ways in which we make use of the various forms of power to which we have access. Having knowledge of how the university works does not necessarily mean I have access to power related to doing my job. I learned this clearly when the pandemic broke out and the dean of the college sent out an email telling faculty that the ITS department would provide us with anything we needed to work from home. "Just ask!" So, I asked, and the answer to my request for an inexpensive piece of software (space in the online virtual world called Second Life) that I needed to continue teaching my course on ethnographic methods was, "we won't support that." When I pushed back on this with the dean, the answer remained a definitive "no" with no explanation. I understood the system, and I understood some of the reservations about Second Life, but it was the only way I could imagine that would allow my students to "meet" others to conduct interviews and learn ethnographic methods. It didn't matter. I had absolutely no power to change the situation, despite understanding how the system works.

Knowledge isn't power, but it can help us gain access to power.

Key Takeaways

- *Power is not simply a negative concept related to obedience and coercion.*
- *Power is something all humans use in all relationships; we live in webs of power relationships that shape what we do and what we know.*
- *Knowledge and power are closely related; power helps us generate knowledge and knowledge helps us to strategically use power, but knowledge alone without access to power is not productive.*
- *Power is dependent upon access to social and symbolic capital.*

CHAPTER 6

Promoting Strong Organizations by Understanding Productive Power

If we return to the DEC example from the beginning of this book, perhaps if the organizational paradigm of the company had been different, leadership would have been more successful in understanding—interpreting—the changing cultural climate. Part of what kept the paradigm from changing quickly was the power-dynamics operating inside of the company. But as I discussed in the previous chapter, this isn't just about the power of individuals to make something happen. Power is in part a property of the environment itself and DEC's engineering-centered and academic-like paradigm made it difficult to respond (use power) quickly to a changing cultural and business climate. In fact, DEC's leadership was in many ways disempowered because their paradigm didn't allow them to see the changes happening around them clearly enough to exert the power needed to effectively redirect the flow of corporate decision-making.

The DEC paradigm had similarities to the paradigm at my university, with its emphasis on debate and discussion. That paradigm works fairly well in the university where faculty have tenure and the importance of responding to the larger cultural context is not so clearly tied to the need to sell things. Tenure is a kind of social and symbolic capital that allows faculty to voice their opinions openly without fear of repression or retribution from administrators, or at least not much fear. At DEC, the prevailing paradigm tended to emphasize the engineering side of what the company did, as I have noted, but the larger context in which DEC was situated had moved to an environment in which there was more focus on making money than on the quality of products sold, and the types of computer products desired by consumers had also changed. Jacob Needham, a philosophy professor at San Francisco State University, observed about the money-centered culture of the 1990s that "[m]oney can buy almost anything we want. The problem [is] that we tend to want only the things that money can buy" (Taylor, 1992). More subtle features of things, such as quality, are often devalued in this type of environment, replaced by a focus on numbers ("data") the meaning of which is often not well understood, but which are often perceived as being translatable into dollars and cents.

In other words, the issue at DEC wasn't simply poor management (although that was also part of the problem) it was a misalignment of values—the engineering/quality emphasis of DEC's operational paradigm did not align well with the larger cultural context in which generating huge shareholder gains and massive profits was the primary value shaping the ideas of many business leaders. It's not that these frameworks are entirely disparate, but the primary values driving decisions at DEC were not aligned with trends of the larger cultural context in which DEC operated and this limited the ability of DEC's leadership to successfully employ power to correct the company's course. Note that I am not taking a position on which value structure is better or worse (although I do have an opinion on this). The key point to take away here is that the problem was one of cultural or value *alignment*. You can be as wrapped up as you want in the issue of your organization's "culture," but if the organizational paradigm isn't aligned with value structures in which the organization operates, there is a good chance that the organization will not succeed. There are some exceptions to this—some organizations, like Greenpeace, are set up to challenge prevailing value structures, so the basis of how they are employing power is different from a company like DEC that wants to sell its products *within* the framework of prevailing cultural flows.

Chapter 6. Promoting Organizations by Understanding Power

When this sort of misalignment occurs, it generates a context in which power is being wielded often in ways unlikely to achieve desired ends or that may be directly at odds with achieving those ends. Leadership at DEC obviously wanted the company to succeed and they were employing various types of power in an effort to make that happen. But their failure to accurately read the larger cultural context in which the company was embedded, which itself was generated in part by the operational paradigm within which leadership was attempting to influence the company's course, led to poor decision-making. The problem with DEC wasn't so much about culture as it was about leadership's poor understanding of a larger cultural context and consequent application of policies and decision-making that would successfully employ power to achieve desired ends.

This chapter is about power and how we use it to achieve institutional aims. In the previous chapter, I presented an exploration of the concept of power that relies on the metaphor of a circuit board. Power is everywhere, and nodes within the network of power relations have variable access to and understanding of how to use the flow of power. One of the things I believe to be important in rethinking the notion of organizational dynamics as having to do with organizational culture is recognition of the fact that we use terms like culture and power in a very sloppy manner. Without careful thinking carefully about the way we use concepts like power and culture their meaning can become so diffuse that they can become effectively useless in broader discourses of organizational dynamics. If the stakeholders in the discourse all have different meanings of these terms, then what are we actually talking about? If the definition of a concept like organizational culture is so vague that it can be expressed as "the way we do things around here" what analytical and intellectual work is it doing?

This matters because anthropological studies of people in various sociocultural contexts have shown an empirical fact that I have been navigating throughout this book: language shapes how we perceive and think about the world. Americans use terms like culture and power frequently, and not particularly precisely, but this should not be taken as meaning people in all sociocultural settings place as strong an emphasis on these concepts as Americans do. Nor should we assume that most Americans are using these terms in corresponding ways with clear meanings—they aren't. One interpretation of the power concept that I believe has become common in American society, and which I mentioned earlier, is that power is negative. When we speak of those "in power" or bosses who wield power, there is often a subtle (and sometimes not very subtle) connotation of a negative association of power with the use of force, poor leadership skills, or simply managers being assholes. But as I've tried to emphasize in this book, power isn't just a negative, coercive or repressive thing that makes us to do things we don't want to do. That can be one way to think about power and, as I discussed in the previous chapter, a key aspect of power is the ability to get people to do things they wouldn't otherwise do. But that does not necessarily mean it is getting them to do things they don't want to do. Power can be used as a tool to bring out desires and to make interests evident and, thus, to align individuals into frames of collective goals. Good leaders are able to employ power to bring people together. And this brings us to a key point of this book. It isn't culture that brings people together in an organization; it's power.

Although the use of power can have negative aspects, power is an inevitable part of social interaction that can be a productive and positive force in any organization—as long as it is understood well and as long as those making decisions recognize and understand the larger social, economic, and political context in which their organization operates. Rather than excluding, repressing, and censoring people, power can produce domains of social interaction that are productive and positive. Individuals gain knowledge through this productive process and can become successful in their organizations if they see this and understand clearly how to strategically use power.

Chapter 6. Promoting Organizations by Understanding Power

PRODUCTIVE POWER

Obviously, power is an important part of social discipline and conformity. It is common for people to talk about others as being "power-hungry" or about the exercise of power as being something that interferes with effective organizational operations. But awareness of the productive capacity of strategically using power can help organizations work better. This chapter focuses on helping leaders (and followers) understand that power is not bad if it is understood and used in productive ways. Power allows managers to get projects done and allows subordinates to engage in their work successfully. If employees in an organization do not feel empowered to accomplish their goals—which can mean either personal goals or organizational goals—then things won't go well. What those leading organizations need to do is consciously create paradigms in which power is understood clearly by all members of the organization.

This brings us to the issue of leadership. I want to take a short detour because a fad throughout the business and educational worlds in the U.S. in recent years has been to talk about the importance of leadership training for virtually everyone in society, it would seem. At the University of Texas, it became almost a cliché that academic administrators were trying to make every program on campus somehow about leadership. This is an example of what happens when "leaders" fail to understand context and misconstrue social interactions in terms of essentialized and simplistic social variables. Leadership is important, but it is only part of a complex picture. An example will help. In the second half of the 20th century, there was a great deal of academic interest in the organizational approaches of Japanese businesses. One of the things that was commonly noted is that people in Japan were promoted and had their salary increased based on time of service and age, rather than merit or ability (this has changed quite a bit in the 21st century) (Allison, 2013). To some extent, this is true, but if you think about the logic of the argument, it doesn't make much sense. Why? Because if it were true, there would

The Myth of Organizational Culture

be no leaders; there would only be groups of people who collectively rise to the top of an organization and become decision-makers. Obviously, some people get promoted in Japan to leadership positions on the basis of ability, with only limited regard to age or time of service. This is an example of seeing only part of a context and then essentializing that element—by this, I mean that one takes a key element of the context and generalizes it in such a way that it over-simplifies what is actually going on in a social context. There is truth to the idea that age and seniority have played a significant role in how Japanese white-collar workers are promoted, but that's only part of the story, the remainder of which tends to get overlooked when that aspect of Japanese organizational dynamics is over-emphasized.

The same problem happens with the way leadership programs often get promoted, because they tend to ignore a key point. If everyone is a leader, who is a follower? I don't mean follower in the sense of people who just do what they are told, but in the sense of people who have a strong understanding of how to function as a contributor to an organization, but not necessarily as a "leader." Of course, leadership gets used in a variety of ways (we always come back to the issue of definitions of terms), so being a leader can mean things like being honest, being good at working with people, listening well to subordinates, etc. In fact, the term is so vague (like the word culture) that it probably isn't of much use. But if you think about it a bit the leadership fad over-emphasizes one element of the complex set of interactions that make up any organization. Leaders exist in and are defined in terms of those they lead—followers. There would be no leaders if there were not people who were good at following directions, carrying out orders, etc. In fact, the relationship between those who lead and those who follow is symbiotic. Figure 4 shows the I ching symbol used in Chinese philosophy to represent the idea that the two components of the world, yin and yang, are intertwined. The black dot in the middle of the white field and white dot in the middle of the black field show that oppositional concepts like good and evil, high and low, young and old, cannot be understood without each

Chapter 6. Promoting Organizations by Understanding Power

other. The concept of good is meaningless if there is no corresponding concept of evil—the presence of the other defines the parameters of each. The same is true for ideas like young and old. It wouldn't mean much to talk about someone being old if we had no concept of what it is to be young.

The broad emphasis on leadership, without corresponding reference to and recognition of followership, representants a failure to understand that leadership itself is defined in terms of those who are led. This raises an interesting question of why don't we have programs in how to be a good follower? The answer is that it's related to cultural values. First of all, the notion of interpenetrating opposites is not a big part of Western philosophy. This is something one sees in East Asian cultures like China and Japan that tend to emphasize the cyclical nature of existence over a linear understanding of the world and view opposites as complementary rather than conflicting. Second, in American society there is a broad value placed on being a leader. Those who lead have symbolic capital and are respected as important contributors. Those who are viewed as followers, a term that often has negative connotations, lack that capital.

The understanding of the relationship between those who lead and those who are led in the U.S. tends to be rather linear and constructed around a hierarchical notion of power rather than the type of concept I've been discussing in this book, where power permeates all aspects of social relationships. This generates a concept of

Figure 4. I Ching symbol used in Chinese philosophy that shows the interpenetration of yin and yang (Wikipedia).

The Myth of Organizational Culture

leadership in the U.S. that is associated with positionality in relation to power, status, and money. It's also associated with another value in American society, that of working well with others. Team players are looked at positively. In fact, this value is so strong that those of us who tend to be introverted or loners can be looked down upon or pitied in many social contexts. American culture places a strong value on being extroverted (friendly, social, outgoing, proactive, etc.). Being a good leader tends to be defined in terms of these types of values. But not all societies place a high value on extroversion. Thus, what it means to be a leader in the U.S. is going to be different from how it is conceptualized in other societies, like Japan, that emphasize different values, such as decorum and respect for others.

Of course, it would be nice if things were this simple, but they aren't. Cultural values shape how we behave, but individual humans have agency and can behave in ways contrary to prevailing value sets or can draw heavily on particular aspects of cultural values that lead to poor behavior in groups. Confidence is highly values in American society, but it can easily morph into arrogance, which usually creates problems in relationships between leaders and followers. As philosopher Aaron James has pointed out nicely, assholes have a way of finding their way into positions of power (James, 2014). James notes that assholes consider themselves to have special value and advantages in relation to others—they often see themselves as better, more intelligent, more moral, etc.—and this generates a sense of entitlement that immunizes them from the feelings, attitudes, and criticisms of others. As a result, assholes easily exercise coercive power as a means to bully and manipulate others which, in turn, tends to generate toxic environments that are difficult for those not in leadership positions to navigate.

In fact, it was precisely this type of situation that helped me decide to retire early from the university where I worked. Rather than attempt to change the situation, it was much easier, particularly in terms of my mental health, to simply leave. Assholes have a way of *forcing* others to do things they wouldn't necessarily do otherwise

Chapter 6. Promoting Organizations by Understanding Power

or to influence them as a result of creating a negative social environment. And this brings us back to the issue of power. Assholes are often pretty good at using power, but the form of power they use is what I refer to as *suppressive power* or a use of power that generates a highly controlled and restrained environment in which those in positions of followership often feel disempowered. This type of power is usually associated with tyrannical or oppressive political and organizational environments where decisions are made by leaders with little or no consideration of how people within the organization will experience the organizational paradigm that is generated as a result of those decisions. Leaders who employ suppressive power are not usually very healthy for the long-term success of an organization, unless those in followership positions buy-in to a strict hierarchical structure with a linear and very top-down approach to the use of power. Americans, in part due to the broader cultural values placed on participatory decision-making, often struggle in this sort of environment.

Suppressive power is not necessarily unproductive. In fact, I think in the case of my retirement, the use of suppressive power was productive from the perspective of the department chair, who clearly wanted me gone. Because I had tenure, he couldn't force me to resign or retire, but many of his actions and comments were overtly aimed at getting me to retire or at least making me recognize I was not valued as a contributor to the department. I acquiesced in deciding to retire early, so from his perspective his actions would probably be classified as a use of productive power. Unfortunately, those same actions characterized much of what happened in the department, generating a toxic work environment and low level of morale among faculty and graduate students. Thus, in the grater scheme of things, that particular approach to employing power wasn't particularly productive. When humans are involved in social settings, it's usually complicated.

Productive power comes from an awareness of these types of prevailing social values and the ability to manipulate the social environment to access those values. This is different from the type of power that is coercive—my boss can make me do something I don't want to do and can fire me if I don't do it. Most people understand that form of power. Productive power arises from the ability to see power as a part of relationships that can be creative and can produce understanding and knowledge. This is an element missing in approaches like cultural training and cultural analysis programs along the lines of the competing values framework developed by Cameron and Quinn, which does not carefully address the role of power in the way interpersonal relations and organizational dynamics function (Cameron & Quinn, 2011). Cameron and Quinn recognize the presence of hierarchical power, but tend to see power in terms of the effectiveness of culture management to control and change an organization rather than as something that permeates all relationships within an organization. Power shapes the organizational paradigm and conscious awareness of how power works in an organization can help to build an operational paradigm that will function successfully within different cultural contexts.

Although I have implied that suppressive power can be negative, there is an important point to keep in mind here, however. The ideas of suppressive power and productive power are not inherently good nor bad. Whether a particular use of power is suppressive or productive is related to the type of organization within which it is deployed. In an environment, like the military, where the organizational paradigm reflects a hierarchical structure in which those of higher ranks are able to give orders that are expected to be followed, the nature of what is experienced as suppressive power will be different from an environment like a university where the organizational paradigm is centered on the notion of collective governance, meaning that department chairs, deans, provosts, etc., are viewed as part of the faculty and, although they have power to make decisions, tenured faculty have considerable leverage to influence those decisions and can even reject them. In a military organization, strong top-down leadership may be necessary and even desirable. Thus, productive

Chapter 6. Promoting Organizations by Understanding Power

power emanates from those who are able to enact decisions through things like giving clear orders and expectations about how those orders will be followed and when it is acceptable to question orders. If the stake-holders in an organization understand its structure, and why it is structured in a particular way, use of power in a way that aligns with the organizational paradigm will be productive. Giving orders in a military environment is not necessarily suppressive and, in fact, may be a productive use of power. Giving orders in a university environment is usually suppressive, because a central value of the typical organization paradigm in American universities, at least, is collective decision-making. Leadership tends to be diffuse and there is a strong expectation that all or most stakeholders will participate in the process of making decisions. This value has led to the creation of structures such as faculty councils and student government that are intended to broaden participation in decision-making.

The key point here is that good leadership is not an objective behavior that we can isolate from the organization within which it is exercised. Good leadership is closely tied to the social and cultural context—within an organization the organizational paradigm—in which individuals who work in that organization operate. Organizational environments that emphasize some form of collective leadership demand a different approach to the employment of power than those more hierarchically structured. Hence, leadership will take on different characteristics in these distinct organizational structures. There is no a right or wrong organizational structure, nor is there a right or wrong approach to the use of power. Rather, the ways we use power need to be aligned with the type of organizational paradigm within which leaders operate. This is very similar to the point made earlier in the book that decision-making needs to align with broader cultural values.

Returning to the issue of assholery, when it comes to leadership, assholes are often those who see themselves as outside of the organizational paradigm in which they are actually embedded and, thus, feel they can exercise power as they see fit, rather than as is appropriate to that organizational paradigm. In some cases, they view themselves as change agents charged with the right to redefine the organizational paradigm in a way that they, personally, believe to be correct without giving much consideration to the thoughts and ideas of others. In my experience with problematic leaders who routinely engage suppressive power, this is a defining feature of their leadership approach and it is normally counterproductive in terms of creating a positive working environment. Thus, we can think of a toxic organizational environment as one in which suppressive power, defined in relation to a particular organizational paradigm, is the primary mode of action on the part of people in leadership positions. Again, I want to emphasize that toxic and positive organizational environments are not objective states. They are products of how leaders engage in the use of power and how that engagement reflects patterns of behavior associated with the overall organizational paradigm in which they operate. Productive power arises when leaders and followers align their behaviors to patterns of behavior expected within an organization.

This presents something of a problem: what if the organization needs to change? Strong organizational paradigms have built-in methods for challenging the system and generating frameworks for change. This is a necessity because no organization operates within a stagnate social and cultural environment. Change is constant and successful organizations are able to react to that change. If an organization lacks built-in structures allowing for the expression of dissent, open debate, and disagreement in decision-making, it can be challenging to use power productively. One of the reasons organizations fail is that stakeholders throughout the organization don't recognize that the productive exercise of power is the key to organizational, and thus individual, success. A circuit board without any power doesn't work. The same is true for any human organization. Without a flow of productive power, the organizational will fail. With too much suppressive power, productive power is drained from the organization and it will begin to falter. Members of any organization

Chapter 6. Promoting Organizations by Understanding Power

need to be able to understand and identify both productive and suppressive forms of power use (behavior) and need to develop structures that allow for the expansion of productive power and reduction of suppressive power.

A successful organizational paradigm normally will need built-in structures for promoting productive power, such as forums for open discussion and debate and means for people in followership roles to question or challenge the decisions of those in leadership roles without necessarily undermining the authority of those in power and without being concerned about or fearful of potential repercussions of voicing critical opinions and ideas. Creating a paradigm in which power is openly understood as a key component of the organization with which one interacts helps in developing the knowledge necessary to building an organizational paradigm that can anticipate and adjust to cultural change and difference. It can also increase success when organizations merge. When DEC and Compaq merged, there was a lot of talk about different corporate cultures that made the transition hard. In reality, these were different organizational paradigms with different power-structures and the two did not mesh well. Greater awareness of this aspect by leaders in both organizations would have helped in the transition process.

KEY TAKEAWAYS

- *Good leaders understand how power works with an organizational paradigm and understand how to employ power productively.*
- *Good leaders understand that power can be used strategically to generate knowledge that will help both individuals and the organization succeed.*

CHAPTER 7

Cultivating an Anthropological Mindset

My first academic job was in an anthropology department at an institution on the West Coast I'll call SoCal University. When I interviewed, I was excited about the possibility of starting my career as an assistant professor in a positive, growing department with what looked like a great future ahead of it. I flew out to California, interviewed for the job, and was offered a position on the spot. I probably should have seen the red flags, because that's not how things usually work in the academic world. The normal pattern is a wait, often of several weeks, before the entire hiring process works its way through interviews and bureaucracies. It is quite unusual to be offered a job during the interview process in academic environments, because that process itself is normally part of the collective governance of a department and needs approvals form higher levels of administration. Decisions related to things like hiring are made by committees, not individuals. That was the red flag, and it should have clued me in to the fact that the department was a dictatorship, not a democracy. But I needed a job, and academic jobs are difficult to come by in fields like anthropology. And Southern California was considered a nice place to live (I didn't like it, actually), so it made sense. I don't think I would take the job knowing what I know today, but I was young and innocent....

When I arrived in sunny Southern California, things seemed very positive. Leaders of the department had applied for and received a significant Federal grant to be used in building the anthropology

Chapter 7. Cultivating an Anthropological Mindset

program and that had been important in recruiting new faculty. In fact, over two years the department had hired six new junior faculty, which is an unusually large expansion for an academic department over a short time. We were a youthful and energized group, excited about what we hoped would become a strong anthropology department. Three years after I was hired, all six of us had departed for other jobs. Most surprising, and telling, was the fact that a professor who had already gained tenure took a non-tenured job at another university, having to start the tenure process again from scratch. All of us had missed a very simple element to the organizational paradigm employed in the department—it was a dictatorship. It's not surprising that we missed this, because most academic departments don't function that way. It was an anomalous situation which, when combined with the scarcity of academic jobs and our overall naivete, mitigated against assessing the organizational paradigm accurately.

I never really understood what was happening in that department or at SoCal University while I was employed there. By my second year, however, I could see that the attitudes and behaviors of departmental leadership were weird, and a bit scary, to say the least. Faculty meetings were held weekly, late on Friday afternoons, which seemed rather odd, since most faculty aren't around on Friday afternoons and faculty meetings rarely occur more than once-a-month in most departments. I have been in some environments where full faculty meetings happen no more than twice a semester, although committees meet more frequently. Stranger still was the fact that voicing of opinions different from those of the married couple who ran the department were met with dirty looks and quick redirection, even overt scolding at times. I was confused about why the dean didn't seem to do anything, because it was clearly what we would call today a toxic work environment. In retrospect, I didn't have the tools to diagnose the situation at the time and I don't think the dean did, either. And because I didn't have tenure, I lacked any real power to resist what was going on. The only option open to the junior faculty in the department was to either suck it up and remain quiet or go back on the market and find a job elsewhere which, in the academic world, usually means moving oneself and one's family to a new place far away and having to start anew.

I was fortunate to find another tenure track position and my wife and I decided it was best to move on. At the end of my last semester, I had an exit interview and told the dean what I thought. He looked surprised and listened carefully. I was among the first to leave the department and after a few more of us went on our merry ways, university leadership removed the department chair and put a professor from another department in their place. It would be easy to claim that the couple who ran the department had created a bad culture. It certainly was a negative work environment. But this is too simple an explanation, because they were functioning in a larger context that permitted their behavior (or at least ignored it) and lacked methods and systems designed to see beyond the outward appearances of success evident in obtaining Federal grant money and hiring a slew of new faculty. As I look back on that first academic job, I can see clearly that an ideology of growth was permeating the university, and the department reflected that ideology and the organizational paradigm that went with it in the way decisions were made. The evidence used to measure success was that growth was happening—the department was expanding, had new facilities, and enrollment was on the rise. In fact, the institution as a whole was growing rapidly when I joined up, with new construction and increased enrollment characterizing the campus, as well as an effort to rebrand the institution with new signage and a new logo.

A central part of the growth focus was a professed ambition by leadership to become a research university and to move away from its identity as a commuter school focused primarily on teaching. The fact that the anthropology department had managed to secure Federal funding to develop the department was a major accomplishment and this gave the chair and their husband leverage (power) with upper-level administrators who responded positively to their leadership. In other words, the couple running the department had secured

Chapter 7. Cultivating an Anthropological Mindset

a fair amount of both social and symbolic capital in obtaining a Federal grant and that gave them power to do as they wished within the department and to be largely left alone by administrators beyond the departmental level. The key point here is that both social and symbolic capital were identified in terms of the larger organizational paradigm that emphasized growth without much thought given to what that meant, beyond more grants, more students, more faculty, and more buildings. Assessment was driven by evidence of accumulation of that capital—a growing department meant success, which was interpreted as evidence of successful leadership. It was not until the department started to shrink that higher level leaders stepped in and questioned the decisions and abilities of departmental leadership.

This makes sense if you think about it. Leaders within an organization normally assess failure and success on the basis of the extent to which results align with goals and values represented through the organizational ideology and paradigm. At SoCal University the driving value within the organizational paradigm was growth. Hence, as long as things were growing, a department and its leaders were considered successful. Should growth be halted or reversed (as it was in the anthropology department), it was time to investigate what was wrong with a department. I doubt higher level leaders ever gave much thought to the fact that their mode of assessment was based on an arbitrary value that had been developed (perhaps even unintentionally) as the core motivating structure of the institution's organizational paradigm. There is nothing inherently good about growth (nor necessarily bad). However, in the U.S., growth is viewed throughout most organizations as an objective and unquestioned good—the economy should grow, businesses should grow, universities should grow, endowments should grow. If an organization is static or shrinking, the assumption often is that there is something wrong with that organization. This seems so natural to Americans that they rarely question the idea that growth is a positive. However, this belief is a cultural value, not an objective truth.

In other societies, it's not necessarily the case that growth is valued as highly as it is in the U.S.—in rural Japan, where I did an ethnographic study of entrepreneurs and small-business owners, I found that most of the people I spoke with were overtly *not* interested in growth of their business (Traphagan J.W., 2020). As one woman told me, growth of her business would mean she'd have to focus more on the administrative side of things rather than running the store (a gelato shop) and interacting with people. She had no interest in growing the business. Zero. She wanted the business to continue because she enjoyed the work and it provided sufficient income for her to live as she wished (which was a rather simple lifestyle). She had no ambitions to pursue options like franchising her business, despite the fact that she often had long lines of customers, which might suggest success to someone focused on growth and expansion. The central value driving her business was not growth, but sustainability. This led to a different sort of organizational paradigm in which any symbolic or social capital generated would not come from a commitment to growth. That organizational paradigm was also embedded in a larger cultural context, that of rural Japan, in which there has emerged a strong interest in building sustainable organizations and institutions in the face of significant population decline, which itself creates a context in which sustained growth is problematic.

When it comes to the situation in anthropology at SoCal University, what was missed, as it often is in higher education, was the fact that the chair (and her husband) lacked leadership skills in relation to working with people even while having skill at obtaining funding. Getting a big grant in a university that wants to grow into a research institution can give someone a deep well of capital that can translate into power. It is a source of prestige, status, and also brings in money in the form of direct costs to be used in programs and indirect costs, usually about an additional 50 percent of the grant value, provided to university administration for overhead expenses associated with administering the grant. If you want to be a star in the eyes of university administrators, bring in Federal grant money.

Chapter 7. Cultivating an Anthropological Mindset

Unfortunately, the department turned into a disaster area because no-one had thought much about how power could, or should, be used to build it. As long as it was growing, things were good. There was no consideration of whether skilled leaders were in place to build the department, nor to what kind of local (college and departmental) organizational paradigm would work best to support and develop a group of young, competent, and motivated new faculty. There was quite a bit of focus on renovating the department offices, but little thought given to the structure of the department, the distribution of power, the decision-making process (well, that was clear, all decisions were made by the couple in charge), nor the best processes and practices to bring new untenured faculty along and ensure that they achieved tenure and remained in the department for many years. In other words, the value of sustainability did not inhabit the organizational paradigm—just the value of growth. Had the value of sustainability been driving decision-making, it is likely the outcome would have looked quite different. But here's the rub, because the larger organizational paradigm built around an ideology of growth dominated the institution as a whole and because that institution was embedded in a society that placed significant emphasis on growth, particularly in the pre–Enron 1990s, it is unsurprising that this outcome would unfold. I would not say it was inevitable—people can push against prevailing values and ideas—but it was predictable.

This chapter is intended to focus on a key element of organizational success—leaders must know the values that drive an organization (not the ones on value and mission statements, but the ones people bring to the table and that shape the organizational paradigm) and they also need to know themselves. I doubt that the couple leading the anthropology department saw themselves as dictators who were attempting to dominate and control the behaviors of new, junior faculty. I wouldn't be surprised if they viewed themselves as mentors and compassionate leaders in building the department. But that was not how they were viewed by the new faculty. Understanding values

The Myth of Organizational Culture

and how they are interpreted, as well as understanding how identity plays a role in that process is different from setting up mission and value statements that may or may not have much to do with the values that truly shape how decisions are made and the directions in which organizations develop. The dictatorship that was the anthropology department at SoCal University was a product not simply of the people who ran the department, it was the product of a context (organizational paradigm) that was primed to generate dictatorships. Why? Because success was measured not on values such as developing workplace morale or understanding power distributions and how to develop good leaders, but on growth. As long as growth was happening, leadership was succeeding. It didn't matter much how they were doing it or how junior faculty members were interpreting that process—until it did, when everyone started to leave.

It is somewhat ironic that within the anthropology department—a field focused on understanding human behavior in groups—there was little understanding of how the organizational paradigm worked, nor much interest in figuring that out. The values of the department were those of the couple in charge; there were few opportunities for competing values and diverse perspectives to be voiced. But this was only part of the problem. Much more important was a lack of awareness among higher-level administrators of how power was used by people in the organization. Thus, there was no structure in place to ensure that there was a conscious focus on developing decision-making processes and allocating power in ways that would support the organization.

Because power permeates every aspect of human social environments, it's important to overtly understand how it works within any organization. Those in leadership positions cannot simply be "in" power, they need to be able to assess power relationships and determine how flows of power will work best to support the goals of organizational leaders. Note an important, but subtle, point I just made. I did not write the "goals of organizations." Organizations do not have goals and do not think. Rather, as anthropologist Mary Douglas

Chapter 7. Cultivating an Anthropological Mindset

argued several decades ago in her book *How Institutions Think*, organizations and institutions provide structure that influences the way individuals within those organizations think and make decisions. They do this by creating a framework or scaffolding through which individuals at all levels interpret and classify the world (business environment, academic environment, political environment, etc.) in which they operate. Organizations help to create a sense of shared categories, or frameworks for interpreting the world and making decisions, through collectivized structures (Douglas, 1986).

It is this framework that I have been calling an organizational paradigm throughout this book. We can also think of this framework as being shaped by ideology, or a system of ideas, beliefs, and values, that structure and limit the content and process of decision-making. Within an organization, this framework often tends to generate a kind of conceptual hegemony in which the ideas and beliefs of those at the highest levels of the organization, and with the most access to power, generate a worldview in which the values of the leadership class becomes widely accepted as the organizational norm, thus creating a status quo in which decisions at all levels algin with those values (Adamson, 2014). This is what happened at SoCal University. High-level leaders wanted to "grow" the institution, without much thought given to what that meant organizationally, and that emphasis on a simplistic model of growth became the defining value behind a hegemonic ideology that permeated much of the organization and shaped not only the decisions made but the assessment of those decisions and their outcomes.

Mission and value statements can help in setting this ideology in place, but, as noted earlier in the book, people don't necessarily react to mission and value statements as leaders wish or expect. Alone, mission and value statements don't amount to much in terms of the overall organizational paradigm, because there are many other variables involved in shaping that paradigm. Often the type of ideology that tends to permeate an organization reflects elements of larger ideological and cultural patterns external to the organization itself.

The Myth of Organizational Culture

When this happens, people are less likely to push strongly against the organizational paradigm, because that paradigm seems natural. In other words, people are less likely to question the idea of a concept like growth as the driving value of an organization if that same value prevails in the larger cultural context in which the organization operates. This is what I mean by the ideology becoming hegemonic; it is so deeply embodied in the minds of individuals as well as the decision-making structure of an organization (which reflects the minds of individuals) that it doesn't get questioned very often. And when it does, as happened in the anthropology department at SoCal University, the structure may struggle and those who decide to resist the hegemonic ideology may be forced to leave or may conclude that departure is their only option if they want to be in a better situation.

A central point to take away here is that the particular values are, themselves, interpreted by people. They have no inherent goodness nor badness. An organization run as a dictatorship can work just fine if the people within the organization are ideologically aligned with that form of decision-making and that type of power structure. In the U.S. dictatorships often don't do well because the prevailing ideology in American society emphasizes some sort of collective involvement in decision-making, or at least some level of attention to the needs of those with limited access to power by those with deep access to it.

Power, itself, is neutral in terms of value. There is no such thing as good nor bad power. Ascription of positive and negative value comes from how it is used within an organizational context and how that use aligns with organizational systems and structures, as well as how it aligns with broader cultural patterns that shape and limit organizational activities. Think of it this way: Gasoline can be used to power both automobiles and tanks. The first can be a productive tool for getting from home to work; the second can be a destructive tool for blowing up your office building. Both involve the use of power. However, the value associated with its use depends on context. If I drive a tank down Main Street and blow up the local pool

Chapter 7. Cultivating an Anthropological Mindset

hall, it's likely to be viewed as a negative use of the power associated with the gasoline running the tank. But if Main Street is in a town that has been invaded by aliens, it's likely to be viewed as an unfortunate, but *positive*, use of the exact same power. The car is no different. If I use my car to commute to work and obey traffic laws, it will be viewed as at least neutral and perhaps positively. But if I speed and cut in and out of traffic lanes, the same commute will be associated with negative use of power running the car or, more likely, it will be associated with the asshole (me) who is using the gasoline. It gets more complex with power and cars, because attitudes about things like environmental protection come into play. Some people might see my use of a 1968 Pontiac GTO to commute as negative because 1968 GTOs get horrid gas mileage and pollute significantly more than modern cars. On the other hand, if I drive a Prius to work some will view it as positive because I appear to be concerned with reducing fossil fuel use. Note that there is no guarantee that such an assumption is true; I might drive the Prius simply because I'm cheap and want to spend less money on gas but couldn't care less about the environment. Or perhaps I find the Prius to be aesthetically pleasing and don't really care about the fact that it uses less gas than a 1968 GTO. It is usually a mistake to assume others share one's values and incorporate them into life in expected ways. Sometimes, this is true, but many times it isn't.

Knowledge of how power works in an organization is essential to assessing the organizational paradigm. Along with this, it is necessary to understand the ideological framework that shapes how that organizational paradigm is built and used. The key to doing this is to recognize that assumptions shape how all of us make decisions, including those at the top of any organization. The first step in understanding an organizational paradigm, which is the first step in trying to assess how to improve the operation and climate of an organization, is to identify and assess assumptions. As a leader, it is essential to regularly engage in a process aimed at recognizing assumptions. This can be done by asking four basic questions:

The Myth of Organizational Culture

1. What assumptions do I and others bring to the table in thinking about how people, in general, should behave?
2. How do personal beliefs influence decision-making and the use of power within the organization?
3. How does my identity influence the perception of others about my role as a leader, the way I make decisions and the decisions I make? How does my identity influence how others think about my use of power?
4. What are the touch-points at which assumptions, identities, beliefs disconnect, or connect, with larger, hegemonic cultural values?

I've used the example of DEC quite a bit throughout this book and I want to return to it again here. As I noted in the discussion of DEC's founder, Ken Olsen, he was often described in terms of humility and a combination of Christian and American values that emphasized integrity and treatment of customers with respect and encouraged freedom to experiment among employees (particularly engineers), which was an important part of his experience as a student at MIT (Kilbane, 2011). His values were part of how he developed the organizational paradigm that characterized DEC and the organizational ideology that influenced the thinking of those who joined the company. This should not be interpreted as meaning everyone just lined up and followed Ken's belief system. However, the approach to decision-making related both to treatment of customers and research and development reflected those values. Early on, Ken no doubt hired people who shared significant elements of his belief system and, in turn, those people hired others who also shared, or at least bought into, the developing ideology and organizational paradigm that became DEC. Of course, as the company grew, the scope of ideas brought into the company became increasingly diverse and the size of the company meant that in additional to the broad organizational paradigm, there were numerous sub-paradigms

Chapter 7. Cultivating an Anthropological Mindset

(such as marketing vs. engineering) that didn't always mesh particularly well. Ken and many of those around him struggled to assess the direction in which the larger society was moving, and, thus, the direction of the computer industry. The organizational paradigm, with its ideological focus on experimentation and debate, eventually no longer aligned with the growth ideology that came to characterize American society in the late 1980s into the 2000s (and which is still a major part of American value systems). This is not to say that growth didn't matter to DEC (or to Ken), but other values were primary, such as engineering quality and integrity, and these became increasingly devalued in American society as the growth value became a hegemonic cultural value. Ken and other leaders in the company held a set of assumptions about themselves, the company, the surrounding social and business environment, and the values that should drive a company. These assumptions shaped the ways decisions were made and had a lot to do with the downfall of DEC.

So, how do we get at the answers to the four questions presented above? Obviously, self-reflection is one way to do this. It's important to think about one's identity and think about how it influences decision-making and attitudes about things like the best way to lead. But self-reflection is limited, since each of us are only one contributor in an organization that often has tens, hundreds, or thousands of contributors each of whom bring their own identities to the organization and each of whom, even if only in small ways, shape the organizational paradigm. Central in assessing how an organization works (and identifying both strengths and weaknesses) is understanding how people think about power—is it a positive or negative force? Attitudes about power are tied with other variables such as personal identities, values, and beliefs. Organizational research focused on understanding how people think about power can help leaders to develop a paradigm and power structure that overtly addresses the needs of the organization and also helps people to understand their relationships to others clearly.

The Myth of Organizational Culture

What Is Research?

Having raised the idea of organizational research, I need to explain what this means, in large part because many people have a rather poor understanding of research and how it works. This is important because there is no more powerful way to understand something than systematic research. Research is the key that unlocks closed doors and helps us to identify and interpret operations of any organization. Unfortunately, the term is used constantly in American society in ways that often do not reflect what research actually is all about. So, I want to begin by explaining what I mean by "research."

We've all done it. I want to buy something like a new car and I tell my spouse/friend/colleague I'm "researching" it on the Internet. Sorry, but when you go to Google and start looking things up, you are not doing research. You are looking things up on the Internet. Research involves clearly defined methods for collecting and analyzing data, as well as an understanding of how to assess quality data as opposed to poor and unusable data. Research is systematic and built around tools intended to identify bias and, to the extent possible, bracket bias off from both data collection and interpretation processes as much as possible. It's unlikely when you look at cars on the Internet you are giving much thought to your own biases about cars and how those biases might influence your decision. Do you ask yourself if you dislike culture X and, therefore, shy away from the cars made in that society, despite the fact that they are good cars? Do you only look at American cars simply because they are sold by American companies while ignoring the fact that the engine of the car you covet may be built in China? Questions that challenge us to think about our own biases are important if any research project is to be successful.

Research is about asking good questions in a systematic way. I'm sure you've heard it said that there are no stupid questions. I don't agree with that. Some questions are poorly constructed or difficult

Chapter 7. Cultivating an Anthropological Mindset

to understand; hence, they are stupid. But stupid questions, or at least very simple ones, are not always bad questions. In fact, sometimes stupid questions can be good questions when trying to understand something that seems obvious to others. I became a master of asking stupid questions when doing ethnographic fieldwork in Japan because it was a useful technique in getting people to talk about things they saw as being too obvious and basic to bother with discussing. People would often engage in a conversation with me around something that seemed simplistic (and stupid), because I was a foreigner and, thus, lacked a sophisticated understanding of the cultural environment. Regardless of whether there are stupid questions, there are most certainly poor questions. These are questions that fail to address a problem, are poorly worded (and thus difficult to interpret), are misleading, or direct the respondent to answer in a particular way. If you want to understand your organization and if you want to understand how power operates within your organization, you have to begin by asking good questions.

Before getting into this, however, we need to ask a very large question: What is scientific research? Americans, in general, have a poor understanding of how science works and what the scientific method involves. Many seem to believe that science provides objective answers to questions or solutions to problems that don't change over time. During Covid, many Americans were frustrated with the CDC and changing instructions on how to react to the pandemic. The problem wasn't the CDC, it was the fact that many Americans have no idea that science doesn't give you *the* definitive answer, but that answers can change as we gain more knowledge and insight through research. Science is a method for learning about a world that is changing, thus it must include methods and ideas that are open to change. Science does not attain truth in any universal sense; it gets small truths that are accepted for a while but that may fall out of favor as we gain more understanding.

Although science operates in a way intended to seek truths, its primary mode of operation is a process of falsification. Science is a systematic way not of identifying what is true, but of identifying what is *not* true. It does this by asking carefully constructed questions designed to help us understand the object of study better by peeling away assumptions and ideas that are false. Note that word, "better." One of the ways to better understand what something is is to understand what it isn't. By peeling away what is false in relation to a problem or context, we get a better sense of that problem or context. But we never get the whole picture or the perfect understanding. There is no objectively best nor perfect understanding, just as there is no objectively best practice in how to understand or how to do something. What is best is temporary and closely related to context, which includes current knowledge. More research means more knowledge which, in turn, means changing understandings of what we observe. In other words, in science all answers are contingent. It's necessary to remain open to the possibility that the answer one has today will change over time as more research is conducted and a better understanding of the world is achieved. Science always circles the bullseye, but doesn't hit it, because the bullseye is a moving target. We can get very close to the bullseye with careful research, but in the end new knowledge will eventually change our understanding of the bullseye itself. One of the core values of science is openness to being wrong. This means that regardless of our confidence in results, we must remain open to the possibility that future research will change how we see things and may even disconfirm what we think is true today.

In short, science is a process for applying systematic skepticism to our experience of the world. This is true in natural sciences as well as social sciences. Because I do quite a bit of research related to space exploration, I am often asked if I believe intelligent aliens exist and have visited Earth. Although I have no evidence, I think it's likely that there are other intelligent species in the universe. But that's just an assumption based on the fact that the universe is vast, and I think it unlikely statistically that our planet is the only place where life emerged and evolved intelligence. As for visiting Earth,

Chapter 7. Cultivating an Anthropological Mindset

I think it's extremely unlikely aliens have visited our planet. There is no material evidence to support the claim that ET has dropped in on us and the distances are so vast that it seems unlikely anyone out there would have visited unless they have access to technologies we don't understand right now. It's not impossible, but I am highly doubtful that our planet has been visited by intelligent extraterrestrials. Should evidence emerge that supports the hypothesis that we have been visited, I will change my tune.

When it comes to understanding social processes, the contingency of scientific knowledge is profoundly important to recognize. We live in a world of constant change (Traphagan J., 2021). This means that the "answers" to our questions about things like organizational dynamics will inevitably change as social contexts change. And we come to another reason why the idea of organizational culture is problematic and why culture change programs often fail or have only limited success. Leaders often assume that by conducting a few surveys or focus group sessions, they can identify the organizational culture, find its flaws, and fix its problems. But an organization isn't a thing; it's a process. This means it is constantly changing, often in unpredictable ways, and that change is driven by the ways in which *individuals* within the organization use power as well as the ways in which the larger social and cultural context in which the organization operates constricts and shapes the flow of change.

THE IMPORTANCE OF POWER AND SELF-AWARENESS

There are numerous ways that can be used in doing organizational research and it is not within the scope of this book to go into details about research and data collection methods. Readers interested in developing skills in conducting research should take a look at any of the numerous books available that focus on qualitative, quantitative, or mixed-methods approaches to research. I am particularly

The Myth of Organizational Culture

impressed by the work of John Creswell and would direct readers to his co-written volume (with Vicki Plano Clark) called *Designing and Conducting Mixed Methods Research* (Creswell & Plano Clark, 2017). Their book is clearly written and covers both qualitative and quantitative approaches to data collection and interpretation.

Rather than working through specific research methods, in what remains of this chapter I'm interested in providing some thoughts that may be useful in developing methods for producing useful analyses of one's organizational paradigm. In the end, if you decide to engage in some type of organizational research program, I encourage you to contact a local college or university and engage people in the social sciences who have a good understanding of research methods. The results will be far more useful than if a project is developed by people with limited understanding of how to collect and interpret.

Indeed, there are many ways to collect and interpret data, and an important first step in doing research is understanding the limits of various research methodologies and knowing how to apply the correct methods for the type of questions one wants to address and the types of problems one wishes to understand. There is little in the research process more important than the mindset that one brings to a project. Without awareness of how to think about data and the process of producing data, results are likely to be unusable. In fact, a great deal of the data produced in our data-driven society is of little value. Whether it's the quick survey I get every time I buy something online, the political questionnaire sent to my house prior to an election, or the customer satisfaction survey I get after paying for a service, much of the data collection is too flawed to produce useful results.

Why? Because for the most part the data collection instruments used suck. That's a strong statement. We collect data so that we can understand our business, customers, organizational dynamics, etc., right? What could be wrong with that? To be honest, a lot, if the process is done poorly. I suspect that virtually every organizational climate survey I've received throughout my career has had significant

Chapter 7. Cultivating an Anthropological Mindset

flaws, largely due to the fact that the people creating those surveys didn't really understand how to go about doing research. Here is an example of a survey question similar to the types of questions often found in things like questionnaires intended to assess workplace environments:

How satisfied or dissatisfied are you with senior-level leadership in our organization?

- Extremely satisfied
- Slightly satisfied
- Neither satisfied nor dissatisfied
- Slightly dissatisfied
- Extremely dissatisfied

This seems like a straightforward question that should be easy to answer, but if you think about it a bit, it isn't. The problem is with the definition of "senior" administration. Do I respond by giving my opinion about the president or provost of the university? What if I think the president is doing a good job and the provost isn't? What if I think leadership of my college within the university is excellent, but general university leadership is terrible (or vice versa)? Or, and this is a significant problem, how do I interpret the meaning of "senior"? If I am a junior faculty member, meaning untenured, then everyone who is tenured is senior to me, which means that the chair of my department is a senior administrator. I have no idea how I would, personally, answer this question because I have different answers depending on what "senior" refers to and which administrators about whom I'm thinking as I answer. If most people responding to this question have the same issue, then the data produced are useless, because as a researcher I have no idea what respondents meant when they selected an answer. And even if most people don't think this deeply into the meaning of the question, as a researcher I have no way of knowing they didn't do that. In short, I have data, but I

The Myth of Organizational Culture

don't know how to interpret the data because I don't know, and can't guess easily, what respondents were thinking when they completed the survey.

Here's another example:

How easy or difficult do you find focusing on your graduate students' career development and wellbeing?

- Extremely easy
- Slightly easy
- Neither easy nor difficult
- Slightly difficult
- Extremely difficult

This question represents a common rookie mistake in writing survey questions. It's what's known as a double-barreled question, because it's really two questions, one of which is about my ability to focus on my employee's career development and the other being about my ability to focus on their well-being. The answer would not be the same for these two questions for me, because although I am concerned with the well-being of my graduate students I do not see focusing on that as a primary part of my role as their professor. But even if I did see that as a central component of my role as a professor, I might have different answers to the two questions. Perhaps I find that the climate of the department/college/university is easy in terms of dealing with my graduate students' career development, but problematic when it comes to dealing with their well-being. In fact, this was precisely the situation I encountered early in my career when I received what appeared to be a suicide note in a take-home exam. I had no idea what to do, because there were no clear processes evident in the organization for dealing with a situation like that. There was support for career development and educational issues that might arise, but not much for mental health issues. Unfortunately, when I called my department chair at the time, he was not able to provide

Chapter 7. Cultivating an Anthropological Mindset

any help in directing me to resources I might access to address the problem. Eventually, I decided to call the university counseling line and explain the situation and that provided a way of addressing the worrisome situation. I think the educational environment of the university and resources for career development at that time were excellent, but the resources for addressing issues associated with well-being were limited and difficult to access. How do I answer that question when the answer for me is simultaneously "extremely easy" and "extremely difficult"? If I take the middle answer of "neither" that does not actually represent what I think; it's just a way for me to deal with the fact that the question stinks and that I can't answer it because it stinks.

The ability to recognize problems like this is essential to doing quality research that can actually be helpful in understanding things like power structures and organizational paradigms (or anything else, really). The problem with these questions is that they were not well thought-out; the author of the survey didn't consider how people might interpret the responses of those who completed it, nor how those interpretations might influence the ability of the researcher to understand and analyze the data collected. The second question has additional issues that would be quite difficult to parse, even if the well-being component were separated from the educational one. Suppose another person answering worked in a department where the chair had instituted a program that focused on student well-being, despite there being nothing at the university level? Without other questions that might bring this out, it would be impossible to figure out why some faculty responded negatively and others positively.

The ability to understand and assess any organizational paradigm depends on bringing to the process what I call an anthropological mindset. This mindset relies on awareness of the fact that interpretation is at the center of how people experience an organizational context (or any context). Efforts aimed at collecting data about an organization are not excluded from this interpretation and the fact that people do constantly interpret their surroundings means extreme care needs to be taken in developing data collection instruments that are likely to generate consistent and understandable results. An anthropological mindset (AM) has at least four primary components:

- Self-Awareness, including awareness of personal biases and the potential influence of one's identity on the research process
- Openness to understanding and carefully considering the logic behind perspectives unlike one's own
- A careful approach to asking questions and thinking about how people interpret questions when trying to conduct organizational research
- Recognition that even if a respondent's analysis of what is right or wrong in an organization differs from that of the researcher, their perspective is not wrong—it is simply different

As I wrote those bullet points, I realized that the initial letter spells the acronym SOAR. I really hate those sorts of banal acronyms that have empty meanings: *You will SOAR in your research if you keep these ideas in mind!* No, you won't. In fact, a better acronym would be SORE, if I could figure out how to make that work, because awareness of these ideas will slow you down and often produce confusing results that are difficult to interpret. But if you persevere and work hard to understand the results produced by quality data, you may actually have the knowledge necessary to make intelligent and informed decisions about your organizational paradigm. And, believe it or not, there is an advantage to confusing results that are difficult to interpret. It turns out that human behavior is confusing and difficult to interpret; thus, complex and confusing results are not necessarily a bad thing, because they may accurately reflect

Chapter 7. Cultivating an Anthropological Mindset

the fact that the context being studied is complex and confusing. Of course, those kinds of results are a bad thing if they are the product of poor research planning and bad questions, like those discussed above, that generate confusing data not because the data reflect a complex social environment, but because they reflect bad questions.

So, let's turn to a more detailed discussion of the anthropological mindset.

SELF-AWARENESS

I already dove into the issue of self-awareness earlier in this chapter, but I want to return here and go a bit more deeply into the issue, because it is essential to the AM. Having an AM is not only important in the process of doing research, but in any attempt to make sense of why other people act and think in the ways they do. There are two components to this: (1) awareness of one's identities and (2) awareness of one's biases. Understanding how identity influences behavior is not only important to collecting data; it plays a significant role in how others broadly interpret one's own behavior and roles in an organization. Suppose I am a manager and want to learn more about how those in my section of the organization think about leadership. If I try to conduct interviews, they are likely to produce nothing of value, because people won't be honest with me. Perhaps you are thinking this is a silly claim. You know your employees and they are honest and forthcoming with their ideas, both positive and negative. Your organizational paradigm encourages debate, so people feel empowered to voice their opinions honestly.

Unfortunately, even in fairly open environments that encourage directness, it is difficult to be certain people will answer honestly about things like leadership behaviors or organizational environments. If someone's job is of value to a member of my group, they are likely to respond positively regardless of what they actually think. Go back to my example from the crazy department I started

The Myth of Organizational Culture

my academic career in at SoCal University. I didn't voice my honest opinion to the dean until I was on my way out—I had already accepted an offer at another university and, thus, was unconcerned about issues like retribution. I also timed my meeting with the dean so that it occurred at the end of my last semester, further avoiding any potential for punishment should my comments get back to the department leadership. Had I not accepted another job, I would not have asked the dean for a meeting. It would have generated too much risk for both myself and my family if I were to be fired. And if the dean had gotten wind of the problems in the department and invited me for a conversation about those issues, I would have simply replied with comments either neutral or somewhat positive. I certainly would not have told him what I honestly thought, because I had no basis on which to trust him, having only met him once or twice in my first year. This is not to say that the dean was untrustworthy. I had no idea. And that was the problem. I had no way to be certain of how negative comments might be interpreted and, thus, how those comments might affect me when heard by someone in a position of power over me. Thus, unless I was in a situation where I had some power—and knowledge that one is leaving generated power—or if I simply didn't care about keeping my job, I would be unlikely to answer honestly.

And even if I had a good experience in the department, there is no way to *know* that my responses on something like a faculty environment questionnaire are the result of my good experiences or the result of my unwillingness to put myself at risk. Basically, *you cannot get data you can trust if you are not aware of how your own identity might influence the data provided by respondents.* What is your position of power in relation to those who might participate? This is a key point.

Another central issue, also tied to power structures within an organization, is allowing for anonymity among those who do respond to any research project you develop. If you do something like interviews or focus groups, this means you, as a leader, cannot

Chapter 7. Cultivating an Anthropological Mindset

be involved in the data collection and cannot know who was willing to do the interviews. If it's survey research, you should not know the names or any identifying information about respondents. One of the most stupid things I encountered at the University of Texas occurred whenever the administration launched a survey of something like faculty satisfaction. They always required respondents to enter their university ID and password to access the survey. This effectively eliminated any anonymity, because it would be possible to trace the IDs of respondents and, thus, connect individuals with specific answers. I never did those surveys, because I wasn't particularly interested in dealing with any fallout from the negative opinions I might express (and I had many). From the perspective of someone trying to understand faculty satisfaction, this is a disaster, because it means those with negative opinions are less likely to respond and, therefore, the results of the research will be biased in a positive direction. Of course, that may well be what those conducting the surveys wanted—confirmation of their beliefs that things in the institution were going well. But if that's what you are looking for, then don't bother with trying to understand an organizational climate or paradigm, because you don't truly want to know what it is.

Awareness of personal bias is central to being able to analyze an organizational paradigm. One's personal beliefs, position within a given organizational hierarchy, and experiences will all shape how one thinks about both the data collection process and the interpretation of data collected. All research is influenced by the biases individuals bring with them to the project. This includes the biases of those responding to questions and those creating the questions. The conclusion to be draw from this point is that our "answers" to the analyses we develop to understand an organizational paradigm are subjective, because they are shaped by the identifies of the stakeholders in the organization and the power structures that shape how the organization functions. This brings me to the last feature of the anthropological mindset I want to discuss here: *when the perspectives of others differ from those in positions of power, those perspectives are not necessarily wrong, but simply may be different.* And, along with this, the ideas of those in power are not necessarily right but may simply represent one way of thinking about how to do things in an organization.

If you truly want to understand how an organizational paradigm works and how to effect changes to that paradigm to achieve specific goals, the place to begin is with yourself and your assumptions. This is at the core of building a solid AM. Your identity as a stakeholder in the organization is the starting point, from which you can develop methods for understanding the identities others bring to the organization and how those identities intertwine with power structures to develop a broad organizational paradigm that shapes behavior and, in some cases, generates a hegemonic ideology that limits how people think and act within the organization. With the understanding of identities, with a well-developed AM, one can develop an understanding of how power relationships influence individuals, groups, and the organization as a whole. As Descartes put it, "I think therefore I AM."

Key Takeaways

- *Poor research methods lead to poor question which, in turn, generate poor data that are not useful in assessing an organizational context.*
- *An anthropological mindset, focused on understanding identity in relation to self and other, is central to doing any type of organizational research.*
- *Developing techniques for researching and understanding how people think about and use power in an organization builds better organizational paradigms.*

CHAPTER 8

Organizations, Culture, and Change

In the town in rural northern Japan where I do most of my academic research, there is a small neighborhood filled with old houses once occupied by samurai lords. I lived in that neighborhood for a couple of years doing the research for my doctoral dissertation in the 1990s and have returned almost annually since. A few years ago, I noticed an interesting development. The town government started providing funds for refurbishing the old houses and created a museum in the hopes of drawing in tourists to help stimulate the weak local economy. The plan worked reasonably well and now they get occasional busloads of people from other parts of northern Japan visiting to learn about the neighborhood.

About ten years ago a guy named Hiroshi, who grew up in that neighborhood, had an idea. Why not start a restaurant to cater to the tourists? He talked to his parents and they decided to use the old samurai house he grew up in to create a restaurant right in the middle of the neighborhood. Hiroshi had worked in restaurants most of his adult life, so he was excited about having his own place. They got some money from the town to renovate the house and bought the equipment (using his parents' retirement savings) needed to run a restaurant. And then they came up with an idea: Why not put a pizza parlor in the old samurai house? So, out in a little town, in a little neighborhood in rural northern Japan, there is a pizza parlor in an old samurai house. It's weird, at least for an American. But the pizza is great. And Hiroshi is very busy. The place is usually packed with customers at lunch—even in the hot, humid summers despite the fact that the restaurant lacks air conditioning.

There are a lot of reasons for Hiroshi's success, not the least of which being that he works incredibly hard. But another major reason is that he correctly assessed the larger cultural climate in which he wanted to place the restaurant. He realized that there was a very strong desire by local leaders to strengthen the economy with tourism. He also realized that a restaurant serving "modern" foods like pizza would attract locals in addition to tourists who might want to eat a more traditional dish. He serves some traditional local foods, as well, and these are the dishes often ordered by tourists. However, to people around town his restaurant is known as a pizza place, albeit one that is culturally attuned, meaning it serves interesting pizzas, such as that old Japanese favorite—mayonnaise pizza.

The restaurant is small, but there is a clear paradigm for their operation. In terms of structure, it's a family business in which Hiroshi's parents help, but he also employs local young people to serve customers. The identity of Hiroshi and his family also play something of a role in the business, because they are descendants of samurai and it is their ancestor's house that is now being used as a pizza parlor. The restaurant also reflects something of Hiroshi's identity in its novelty—having been in the restaurant industry, he was interested in creating something new and innovative that would satisfy his personal desires to do something interesting and satisfying with his career. Hiroshi is another local businessperson from that area who has no interest in growth of his business—he wants sustainability. In fact, it would be difficult to see how the business could expand, because its very nature and concept are tied into the samurai history of his family and the village.

The paradigm of Hiroshi's restaurant (I'll just call it Hiroshi's Samurai Pizza or HSP) also involves an awareness of community/government interests and, of course, an awareness of what people want to eat. Government leaders in the town have been focused on finding ways to create a sustainable economy in the face of declining

Chapter 8. Organizations, Culture, and Change

population throughout the region (and throughout Japan). Local leaders have found a variety of ways to do this, including getting Toyota to build a manufacturing plant in the town several decades ago. Hiroshi's vision for HSP aligned well with the interests of town political leaders to turn the village into a historical preservation district. To that end, they built a visitor center (which looks like a traditional building from a couple hundred years ago) and renovated some of the original structures in the village along with Hiroshi's family abode/restaurant. There are also tight restrictions on what can be built for new housing in the village, particularly in terms of the exterior aesthetics of any construction.

Hiroshi had an original idea that empowered him to build a successful restaurant by working the social relationships and his own well of symbolic and social capital very astutely. His samurai ancestry was a source of symbolic capital that helped local politicians to respond positively to Hiroshi's plan, as did his family's ownership of an original building that could be repurposed as a restaurant. He also had social capital as a result of his experience in the restaurant industry—he worked for a large restaurant chain that went bankrupt, leading to his decision to start his own restaurant. Hiroshi understood the larger cultural environment and he knows how to make use of it strategically to help his business succeed. Hiroshi created a model that works; and he created it by understanding the larger cultural environment in which he started his business.

Hiroshi brought together a set of variables—awareness of social context, his own identity, and creativity—to generate an organizational paradigm for his restaurant that has been successful. His restaurant does not *have* a culture; it has an organizational paradigm that is situated within a cultural context and takes advantage of that context to provide an appealing product to consumers. Not only is the organization part of that context, but Hiroshi himself is, as well. Put another way, Hiroshi was able to employ productive power (symbolic and social capital) to get political leaders to support something they might have not otherwise supported in the unusual idea to create a pizza parlor in an old samurai house. It's an odd combination, but it feeds into desires of politicians in the town to build a tourist industry around a historical preservation district while also supporting the creation of businesses that appeal to local residents. This is precisely what I mean when I talk about productive power. All of the stakeholders surrounding HSP are accessing and using power as a means to achieve specific and overlapping goals. The goals line up because Hiroshi assessed the larger cultural context in which he wanted to build a business astutely and was able to develop a theme to his restaurant that fit well into that context. On a much smaller scale, it is basically the exact opposite of what happened at DEC.

What matters here is context and understanding context. The notion that an organization has a culture mistakenly constructs that organization as though it has an existence independent of the larger cultural flows within which it is embedded and the individual identities of those who work for and interact with members of the organization. This is a very complex process, because on the one hand hegemonic ideological structures that help to shape the organizational paradigm have a way of restricting or constricting the ideas and behaviors of people within the organization while, as people interpret and contest organizational values and policies, they influence and change the organizational paradigm through their own behaviors. *An organization is not an object with a culture; it is a process with a paradigm that shapes the way it flows. That paradigm is constantly being shaped by the individual stakeholders who inhabit it.*

Indeed, individuals matter in this process. At the university where I worked for almost 25 years, one of the core values espoused is responsibility, which is defined as meaning "to serve as a catalyst for positive change in Texas and beyond." It's good that administrators defined what they meant by the term "responsibility" because it's a rather idiosyncratic way of thinking about the concept. In fact, it is quite different from my own way of thinking about what it means to be responsible. I associated the word "responsibility" with

Chapter 8. Organizations, Culture, and Change

accountability and duty, rather than with being a catalyst for change. One can be responsible and be committed to the values associated with an organization without being interested in changing that organization. Indeed, there is a curious assumption in this statement—that change is *necessarily* a good thing and that we should always be pursing change. This idea was so prevalent at the University of Texas that we were constantly having to assess programs and make changes, even if it appeared that a particular program was working quite well.

The idea that change is a constant aspect of organizations is a fact. The idea that change is inherently good is a value judgment. And one of the major problems with the "change is good" mindset is that it ignores the question of how we define change and assign meaning to it as positive or negative. I suspect the interpretation of change as positive or negative can be quite different from one member of the university community to another. From my perspective, the majority of changes I witnesses at UT over the last ten years of my time there were negative. Obviously, those in leadership positions would disagree with me (if they didn't those changes would not have been made). Returning to the issue of change as a responsibility, even if most members of the university agree that responsibility is an important value, many may not agree with what it means to take responsibility or agree that the definition presented by organizational leaders represents their own ideas about responsibility.

To further complicate things, people may contest "common" values while maintaining their commitment to the success of the organization and their loyalty to leadership. Contesting behavior can be obvious like open disagreement. But it also can be quite subtle such as a manager quietly reshaping a project to reflect their personal beliefs about how things can be best accomplished in a way that aligns with the organizational paradigm. Keep in mind that the organizational paradigm is *always* interpreted by those who operate in relation to that organization. It is not neutral, and behaviors need to be understood as they relate to the ways in which people are interpreting that paradigm. Contesting behavior can be evident in things like rise in absenteeism or overt complaints about decisions made by leaders during conversations at lunch. The decision to miss work or complain due to unhappiness with leadership is an effort to engage power to achieve one's ends or support one's interests. This should not be viewed as inherently negative, because a loyal employee may well complain about the decisions of leaders precisely be*cause* they are committed to the organization and feel that the direction that leadership is moving is wrong.

I did this several times in my career, but it was almost always interpreted incorrectly by those in power. The voice of resistance or disagreement usually was viewed as evidence of disloyalty. And I got in trouble over voicing my opinion not a few times—the fact of tenure allowed me to be honest and vocal about my ideas without significant repercussions (although I do think it had a negative influence on my career in some ways), and I would not have likely voiced those contesting opinions so openly without tenure. From my perspective, this is exactly where leadership often failed. With some important exceptions, I found disagreement was usually interpreted as disloyalty. This brings us to the key reason why the idea of organizational culture is so problematic—it creates the false image that because an organization has a successful or positive "culture" and values have been codified to bring people together, its members are aligned in the way they think and generally agree with way the organization operates.

Reality is quite different.

Even values espoused specifically to bring people together may not necessarily function that way. For example, Build-A-Bear Workshop states that it views "Di-bear-sity" as a core (Rossi, 2015). This seems like an optimistic way to emphasize commitment to DEI initiatives and to promote an organizational paradigm in which diversity is valued. However, it's fairly easy to imagine that while some might view this as a cute and positive representation of the value of diversity, others might respond that the term trivializes real issues

Chapter 8. Organizations, Culture, and Change

related to diversity in the workplace and more generally in society. Employees might be divided on this point while retaining an overall commitment to the company and even feeling appreciative of the effort despite its weaknesses. Some research has found that rather than making everyone feel included, praising diversity can make some people feel singled out or even threatened (Apfelbaum, 2016). It's not simple.

And this brings us to an important point that is a central takeaway from this book: *The attempt to unify an organization by creating a "culture" is ultimately an exercise of power and people will react to that expression of power in different ways depending on the extent to which the values associated with the desired (by leadership) organizational culture resonate with their personal beliefs.* Of course, the same could be said for any attempt to create an organizational paradigm. Part of the reason I want to veer away from the use of the term "culture" in relation to organizations is that it is definitionally vague. Another reason is that within the world of organizational dynamics, the terms has come to mean something inherently unifying in an organization. This is misguided, because culture is not a set of (marginally) shared values; it's a web of power relationships in which people are embedded and that they use to meet personal and collective goals but that can also restrict their ability to achieve goals. The same power relationships can function to pull people together or pull them apart. How those function will be related to a complex interplay of differential access to resources like social and symbolic capital, which are themselves connected to things like ascribed and assumed individual identities and perceptions about the collective identity of any organization. This is not avoidable, but it can be analyzed and understood. The most important point here is that differences in access to and use of power influence how we respond to and think about values espoused as being shared by members of a group.

Reliance on the culture concept as a way to create unity can mislead those in positions of power into thinking that the core values expressed by leaders of an organization are actually uncritically

The Myth of Organizational Culture

accepted by employees (Henderson & Traphagan, 2005). This can create false beliefs that publicly expressed conformity with corporate values reflects personal acceptance of those values. It also obscures the fact that people may align themselves with core values not because they agree, but because they see other values, like job security, as more important to achieving their personal goals. In other words, the idea that unity can be generated among employees by fixing or creating an organizational culture relies on a naïve assumption that culture unambiguously brings people together and the mistaken belief that organizations can have cultures that are somehow independent of the larger contexts in which they operate. But the reality of culture is that it represents a tremendously complex variable that can both bring people together and pull them apart—or do both at the same time.

So, at this point I expect readers are asking how is the idea of an organizational paradigm different from what I just described? Don't the same problems exist for an organizational paradigm? They do. Any organizational structure—regardless of what we call it—is going to be embedded in larger cultural flows that shape the nature and operation of that structure. This is unavoidable. The value in thinking in terms of organizational paradigms over organizational cultures comes in the fact that a paradigm represents a model. It isn't the way we do things here—which implies something ossified and not particularly open to change. I mentioned the historan of science, Thomas Kuhn, early in this book. He coined the contemporary usage of the term paradigm, particularly as it relates to scientific practices. For Kuhn, a paradigm is a recognized and agreed upon set of accomplishments that provide a model to be used in moving forward or in solving problems identified by a community of practitioners. A paradigm defines things like what should be observed, scrutinized, as well as the types of questions that should be asked in assessing the object of interest. It also identifies how questions should be structured and asked and how to go about interpreting the answers we get to our questions.

Chapter 8. Organizations, Culture, and Change

I can hear readers arguing that this is nothing but a semantic difference. I am sensitive to this critique, but I think that there is more going on here. First, semantics matter. I would argue that the word culture is so vaguely defined and so diffuse in meaning as it is employed in organizational studies, that it does very little intellectual work. Beyond that, the ways the term is employed rarely captures the fact that culture is not necessarily a unifying feature of an organization. Culture (or ideology) can be a homogenizing feature of an organization, because it can create a sense that people think and do things in the same way within the organization. But homogenization is an ideological process that basically forces people into behaving in a way that upper levels of leadership want. It is not an indication that there is any real unity among the members of the organization. It is not an indication of what people truly think; it's an indication of how well they represent what they think in ways that appear to align with the interests and expectations of those at the top of an organization. Shifting to another term, like organizational paradigm, is an approach that recognizes the fact that the ways organizations operate are dynamic and involve the cultural values individuals bring to the organization as well as the fact that any organization is not a stand-alone culture—it is part of a larger cultural context.

This brings me to my second point: Use of the culture concept for organizations tends to blind us to the fact that any organization is embedded in a larger context. Instead of thinking of their organizations as *having* cultures, leaders need to rethink the nature of their organizations and the role of leadership by thinking of culture as a complex variable that works *on* organizations and employees. The influence of cultural dynamics on an organization can be profound, as was the case with DEC, and disastrous if leaders and others within the organization fail to recognize that: (1) their organization is embedded in a larger context and (2) that said context can profoundly shape the ability of the organization to succeed. If leaders recognize that culture is something that works on an organization,

The Myth of Organizational Culture

rather than something the organization possesses, and that cultural values can both bring people together and pull them apart, they will do a better job of creating paradigms of operation that foster individual and organizational success. I see at least for primary steps necessary to accomplishing this:

1. Recognizing that organizations are embedded in cultural contexts that can profoundly shape organizational success and developing an understanding of those contexts as they relate to the organization
2. Seeing that organizational paradigms are products of power relationships
3. Accepting that power can be both productive and counterproductive, depending on how it is used within a particular organizational paradigm
4. Understanding that how power relationships are perceived and strategically used can deeply influence the success of an organization

When leaders embrace these four ideas, they are more likely to develop policies and create an organizational paradigm that can help people understand and react to both internal and external change. Change is a constant; it's the only constant. Change happens because human relations are about power and the strategic use of power. This generates knowledge in the form of new ideas, new values, disagreements over what is normal and natural, and agreements on how to proceed despite the inevitable presence of competing and contrasting ideas and values. As long as the circuit board is functional and turned on, power is flowing through it and all of the different nodes on that circuit board are engaged in that flow of power in various ways.

A successful organizational paradigm isn't one that reacts to change, but one that embraces change by acknowledging the constant

Chapter 8. Organizations, Culture, and Change

presence of power and open and acknowledged building frameworks for people to engage in the productive use of power. Its leaders recognize that power can be used productively to shape the flow of change, but that change is going to be there regardless of what they do because all organizations are limited by the cultural contexts in which power is being exerted not just on individuals, but on organizations as a whole. Overt things like regulations are cultural products. When the president in the U.S. changes, the regulatory environment often changes and that affects organizations. But other cultural trends influence organizations, such as perceptions about what is good or bad—is going green good for society, good for business, bad for business? Organizations exist in contexts of competing values and they need to be able to build paradigms that can assess those contexts and work within the frameworks of change around them. In short,

Culture cannot be contained within an organization. Any organization is part of and a product of the larger cultural context in which it is born and grows.

When we think about organizational "culture," perhaps no example seems more characteristic than IKEA. An international powerhouse with more than 400 stores operating in more than 40 countries, the leadership at IKEA are very aware of the cultural differences visible in the diverse countries where the stores operate. To deal with the problem of different cultures coming together in the IKEA organizational environment, the company uses several techniques, such as an online quiz to find out if you are a good fit to work at IKEA. I'm not. At the end of the quiz (which I've taken more than once) I was informed that it, "looks like you may not be comfortable in the IKEA culture." But IKEA is really a conglomeration of people from different cultures who are brought together and asked to *accept* a particular organizational paradigm. In one of the company's YouTube videos interviewing employees about working at IKEA, there

The Myth of Organizational Culture

is a constant theme of culture and values as essential parts of being an IKEA employee. The people in the video talk about the value of finding new, efficient "smarter" ways of doing things, teamwork, and being "down to earth." And a theme that runs throughout is multicultural diversity. This is contradictory. How can there be an agreement on teamwork and being down to earth while also maintaining respect for cultural diversity and for people who may not necessarily even have a concept of what it means to be down to earth? Is that the American version of the phrase or the Swedish one? Are they the same?

The video confuses culture with IKEA's organizational paradigm and represents them as basically the same thing. But there really are two things going on. First, IKEA has an organizational paradigm that emphasizes teamwork, efficiency, and multiculturalism. The company also recognizes that its employees come from and represent many cultures that are different, but they need to cooperate for the company to succeed. Oddly enough, I value all of these, but still am not deemed appropriate as an employee because I don't fit the professed culture. What, in fact, is going on is that IKEA has a clear organizational paradigm that encourages employees to put the organizational *aims* (presented as values) of efficiency and teamwork ahead of their personal, cultural traits. It is a brilliant strategy leaders at IKEA have developed to *basically take the culture out of the organization* by emphasizing a paradigm of operations that overrides diverse cultures carried by its employees. And it has been quite successful in building an organizational paradigm that is able to cross cultural contexts. I am not making a value judgment here about IKEA. I am simply noting that they have used the culture concept effectively to create an organizational paradigm that downplays cultural difference while at the same time emphasizing openness to diversity.

In the end, understanding this aspect of IKEA is helpful in more deeply seeing the relationship between organizations and paradigms. It helps us recognize how larger cultural contexts can be managed

Chapter 8. Organizations, Culture, and Change

through understanding and building an organizational paradigm that: (1) is alert to and understands how to build good power relationships, (2) is aware of the larger cultural context in which the organization operates and continually builds its paradigm, and (3) is able to leverage larger cultural contexts to support and help in building the organization over time.

IKEA has used the culture concept to create an organizational paradigm that is able to mesh with different cultural contexts (Jacobs & Crockett, 2021). It isn't the only company to have accomplished this feat. In fact, one very old company has managed this for some time. Avedis Zildjian Company produces cymbals and is one of the oldest family-owned companies in the world, having been in business for about 400 years. Zildjian represents an excellent case of how an organization can adjust to change over a very long period of time—the company was originally founded in Turkey and moved to Massachusetts in the 19th century. It started by making noise-makers for the military and today it is the largest maker of cymbals in the world. Zildjian makes cymbals for classical, rock, and jazz musicians. Whatever Zildjian is, it has managed to adjust to changing cultural contexts remarkably well over the course of four centuries and across two continents by building an organizational paradigm (probably multiple paradigms over time) that is flexible and, thus, can react to cultural changes not only in political and cultural environments, but also in musical styles. What Zildjian has been able to do for a long time is assess the context in which it operates and produce musical instruments that are desired by percussionists. The cymbals change over time, with new approaches to making them and new formulas for the metals used and these cymbals reflect as well as influence creative innovations happening in the music world. Imagine for a moment if the leaders of Zildjian centuries ago were convinced that no-one would ever need a "noise maker" outside of the military. The company probably would have gone the way of DEC. Something about its organizational paradigm prevented those running the company from missing the fact that the context within which they do business constantly changes. Indeed, over the years Zildjian has adjusted to the context and in 2010 acquired Vic Firth Company, which makes drumsticks (among other things) and in 2018 the Mike Balter Mallet company. Sticks and mallets are essential to how many percussion instruments are played, so this is a logical expansion of the company's business.

Organizational paradigms shape the flow of change and are shaped by the flow of change in an organization, and that flow is not necessarily in the control of leaders (Cocks, 2022). They are comprised of individuals who interpret and react to their context and those individuals bring their own cultures and identities to the table as they function within the context of an organization. The organizational culture concept is a delusion that has oversimplified this process and overshadowed the role of power in shaping what an organization does and how its stakeholders experience their roles within the organization. It's time we move on from this concept and develop more nuanced and careful ways of thinking about how organizations work.

Key Takeaways

- *Change is a constant and organizations need to be focused not so much on managing change but embracing it.*
- *Change happens because power is at the center of all human interactions.*
- *Organizational paradigms need to be built around the idea that change is unavoidable but that understanding power relationships can help in building the knowledge needed to succeed in ever changing cultural and organizational contexts.*
- *Good organizational paradigms show deep awareness of the larger cultural contexts in which they operate.*

Works Cited

Adamson, W.L. (2014). *Hegemony and Revolution: Antonio Gramsci's Political and Cultural Theory.* Brattleboro, VT: Echo Point Books and Media.

Allison, A. (2013). *Precarious Japan.* Durham: Duke University Press.

Alvesson, M., & Sveningsson, S. (2024). *Changing Organizational Culture, 3rd Edition.* London: Routledge.

Apfelbaum, E. (2016, August 8). *Diversity and Inclusion.* Retrieved November 2024, from Harvard Business Review: https://hbr.org/2016/08/why-your-diversity-program-may-be-helping-women-but-not-minorities-or-vice-versa.

Barbour, H. (2015, April 30). *Corporate Culture: What's All the Fuss About?* Retrieved November 2024, from LinkedIn: https://www.linkedin.com/pulse/corporate-culture-whats-all-fuss-hilton-barbour/.

Bennett, J.G. (1979). A Note on Locke's Theory of Tacit Consent. *The Philosophical Review, 88*(2), 224–234.

Blackbourn, D. (2007). *The Conquest of Nature: Water, Landscape, and the Making of Modern Germany.* New York: W.W. Norton.

Bourdieu, P. (1977). *Outline of a Theory of Practice.* New York: Cambridge University Press.

Cameron, K.S., & Quinn, R.E. (2011). *Diagnosing and Changing Organizational Culture: Based on the Competing Values Framework.* San Francisco: Jossey-Bass.

Carayol, R. (2012). *Why Culture Is More Important Than Strategy.* Retrieved February 2021, from Management-Issues.com: https://www.management-issues.com/opinion/6576/why-culture-is-more-important-than-strategy/.

The Centre for Computing History. (n.d.). *Home.* Retrieved June 2024, from https://www.computinghistory.org.uk/pages/3971/There-is-no-reason-anyone-would-want-a-computer-in-their-home/.

Cocks, A. (2022). *Counting the Dance Steps: Rethinking How We Define, Measure, and Change Organisational Cultures for the Good of All.* Leeds: Conflux Publishing.

Creswell, J.W., & Plano Clark, V.L. (2017). *Designing and Conducting Mixed Methods Research, Third Edition.* Thousand Oaks, CA: Sage Publications.

Dahl, R.A. (1957). The Concept of Power. *Behavioral Science: Journal of the Society for General Systems Research, 2*(3), 201–215.

DeGeorge, R.T. (2015). *A History of Business Ethics.* Retrieved May 2024, from Markkula Center for Applied Ethics: https://www.scu.edu/ethics/focus-areas/business-ethics/resources/a-history-of-business-ethics/.

Works Cited

Douglas, M. (1986). *How Institutions Think*. Syracuse: Syracuse University Press.
Dowie, M. (1977, October). *Pinto Madness*. Retrieved May 2024, from Mother Jones: https://www.motherjones.com/politics/1977/09/pinto-madness/.
Eagleton, T. (1991). *Ideology: An Introduction*. London: Verso.
Eagleton, T. (2024). *Ideology: An Introduction*. London: Verso.
Easton, D. (1981). *The Political System: An Inquiry Into the State of Political Science, 3rd Edition*. Chicago: University of Chicago Press.
Edwards, W. (1989). *Modern Japan Through Its Weddings: Gender, Person, and Society in Ritual Portrayal*. Stanford: Stanford University Press.
Foucault, M. (1991). *Discipline and Punish: The Birth of the Prison*. London: Penguin.
Foucault, M. (1998). *The History of Sexuality: The Will to Knowledge*. London: Penguin.
Gold, A. (2024, April 4). *The History (and Tragedy) of the Ford Pinto: Everything You Need to Know*. Retrieved May 2024, from MotorTrend: https://www.motortrend.com/features/ford-pinto/.
Graziano, M. (2023). *Ignite Culture: Empowering and Leading a Healthy, High-Performance Organization from the Inside Out*. San Jose: KeenAlignment Press.
Green, L. (1988). *The Authority of the State*. Oxford: Oxford University Press.
Hare, B., & Woods, V. (2013). *The Genius of Dogs*. New York: Plume.
Henderson, J.N., & Traphagan, J.W. (2005). Cultural Factors in Dementia: Perspectives from the Anthropology of Aging. *Alzheimer Disease & Associated Disorders, 19*(4), 272–274.
Jacobs, J., & Crockett, H. (2021). *Designing Exceptional Organizational Cultures: How to Develop Companies Where Employees Thrive*. New York: Kogan Page.
James, A. (2014). *Assholes: A Theory*. New York: Vintage.
Kilbane, D. (2011, December 2). *Ken Olsen: Faith, Work, and Charity Support a Computing Career*. Retrieved November 2024, from ElectronicDesign: https://www.electronicdesign.com/technologies/embedded/article/21795617/ken-olsen-faith-work-and-charity-support-a-computing-career.
Koch, A., Brierley, C., Maslin, M.M., & Lewis, S.L. (2019). Earth System Impacts of the European Arrival and Great Dying in the Americas After 1492. *Quaternary Science Reviews, 207*, 13–36.
Kuhn, T.S. (1996). *The Structure of Scientific Revolutions, 3rd Edition*. Chicago: University of Chicago Press.
Labov, W. (2014). *Dialect Diversity in America: The Politics of Language Change*. Charlottesville: University of Virginia Press.
Levine, D.S. (1997, October 27). *Intel, DEC Settle Alpha Chip Dispute*. Retrieved May 2024, from https://www.wired.com/1997/10/intel-dec-settle-alpha-chip-dispute/.
Margenau, H. (1950). *The Nature of Physical Reality*. New York: McGraw-Hill.
Margenau, H. (1961). *Open Vistas: Philosophical Perspectives of Modern Science*. New Haven: Yale University Press.
Mayberry, M. (2023). *Culture Is the Way*. Hoboken, NJ: John Wiley & Sons.
Murayama, M. (1975). *Studies in the Intellectual History of Tokugawa Japan*. Princeton: Princeton University Press.

Works Cited

Peters, T.J., & Waterman, Jr., R.H. (1984). *In Search of Excellence*. New York: Harper & Row.

Pontefract, D. (2015, July 9). *There Is Nothing Wrong with the Term "Company Culture."* Retrieved June 2024, from Forbes: https://www.forbes.com/sites/danpontefract/2015/04/22/there-is-nothing-wrong-with-the-term-company-culture/?sh=7d909fd0dddd.

Richards, E. (1989, April 11). *Sun Microsystems Escalates the War of the Workstations*. The Washington Post.

Ro, S.-h. (2021). *Neo-Confucianism and Science in Korea: Humanity and Nature, 1706–1814*. London: Routledge.

Robertson, J. (2018). *Robo Sapiens Japanicus: Robots, Gender, Family, and the Japanese Nation*. Oakland: University of California Press.

The Role of Education. (n.d.). Retrieved May 2024, from Monticello: https://www.monticello.org/the-art-of-citizenship/the-role-of-education/#:~:text=Thomas%20Jefferson%20believed%20only%20educated,partially%20achieved%20his%20larger%20goals.

Rossi, H.L. (2015, March 13). *7 Core Values Statements That Inspire*. Retrieved December 2024, from Fortune: https://fortune.com/2015/03/13/company-slogans/.

Schein, E.H. (2010). *Organizational Culture and Leadership, 4th Edition*. San Francisco: Jossey-Bass.

Steinberg, J. (1978). *Locke, Rousseau, and the Idea of Consent: An Inquiry into the Liberal-Democratic Theory of Political Obligation*. Westport: Praeger.

Taussig, M. (2018). *Mimesis and Alterity: A Particular History of the Senses*. London: Routledge.

Taylor, B. (1992, January-February). *Crime? Greed? Big Ideas? What Were the '80s About?* Retrieved September 2024, from Harvard Business Review: https://hbr.org/1992/01/crime-greed-big-ideas-what-were-the-80s-about.

Traphagan, J.W. (2004). *The Practice of Concern: Ritual, Well-Being, and Aging in Rural Japan*. Durham: Carolina Academic Press.

Traphagan, J.W. (2013). *Rethinking Autonomy: A Critique of Principalism in Biomedical Ethics*. Albany: State University of New York Press.

Traphagan, J. (2015, April). *Why "Company Culture" Is a Misleading Term*. Retrieved June 2024, from Harvard Business Review: https://hbr.org/2015/04/why-company-culture-is-a-misleading-term.

Traphagan, J.W. (2020). *Cosmopolitan Rurality, Depopulation, and Entrepreneurial Ecosystems in 21st-Century*. Amherst, NY: Cambria Press.

Traphagan, J. (2021). *Embracing Uncertainty: Future Jazz, That 13th Century Buddhist Monk, and the Invention of Cultures*. Manotick, Ontario: Sumeru Press.

Webster, L. (2017). *Will the Corvair Kill You?* Retrieved May 2024, from Hagerty Media: https://www.hagerty.com/media/videos/will-the-corvair-kill-you/.

Wexler, B. (2008). *Brain and Culture: Neurobiology, Ideology, and Social Change*. Cambridge: MIT Press.

Index

Abrahamic religions 27
anonymity and research 138–139
anthropological mindset 135–140
Arrival (film) 29
Asia 35
assholes 110–111, 113; as change agents 114
assumptions 126–127, 130, 140
authoritarianism 21
authority 98–91; and coercion 89; and legitimacy 89
auto industry regulations 53
Avedis Zildjian Co. 153–154

Barbour, Hilton 20
baseball 32–33
belief systems 126
bias: personal 128, 137; in research 139
Boston 32, 80–81
Boston Red Sox 33, 71
Bourdieu, Pierre 76, 94; idea of fields 78
brain and modeling 29–31, 44, 76, 81
Brooklyn Dodgers 32–33
Build-a-Bear 146
business ethics 51

Cameron and Quinn 112
capital *see* social and symbolic capital
change 9, 20, 56–57, 114, 145, 150–151, 153; and science 129
Chen, Julie 58
Chevrolet Corvair 51, 54–55, 72
China 34
coercive power 89, 110
cognition 29–31, 80–81; and dogs 30–31
collective governance 69, 112, 116
collectivism 62–63
collectivized structures 123

college and university: perspectives about 73–74
colonization 88
Confucianism 34
construct 44
context: business 54; cultural and social 54, 56–57, 60, 82, 94, 124, 143–144
contingency 3, 71
counting 27–29
Creswell, John 132
critical thinking skills 4, 75, 96
cultural change 57
cultural learning: church and school 65
cultural lens 42
culture 2, 3, 8–10, 16–18, 66–67, 75–76, 106, 140, 147–149; and algorithms 64; as bounded 36, 43; as cascading system 46–47; and language 64; and physical objects 36; as process 23, 43–45; and rules 31; training 65

Dahl, Robert 88–89
data 104, 128, 132–135, 137
decision-making 56, 92, 103–105, 121, 123–124; evidence based 131; and personal beliefs 126
definitions 25, 70–71
DEI 60, 146–147
determinism 77, 80
dialect 80–81
Digital Equipment Corporation (DEC) 5, 6–10, 13–16, 103–105, 115, 126–128, 144, 149, 153
discipline 93
dogma 11–12
dognition 30
double-barreled questions 134–135
Douglas, Mary 122

159

Index

Eagleton, Terry 70–71
Eastern culture 34
efficiency 69, 72–74
Einstein, Albert 77
embodiment 26, 76, 78
English 28–29, 62
Enron 17–18
entrepreneurialism 3
essentialization 108
ethics 51–52, 54–56
ethnocentrism 2, 35
expectations 47–48

feedback 77
Fenway Park 32
Ford Motor Company 52–54, 56–57, 60; Pinto 52–53
Foucault, Michel 92–94

General Motors 52, 54–57, 60
Goldman Sachs 22
government standards 53
greed 50–51
Green, Leslie 89
growth ideology 118–122, 127, 142

habitus 76–83
Harvard University 74
hierarchy 40, 69, 101, 112–113
Hiroshi's Samurai Pizza 141–144
Human Dimensions of Organizations (HDO) 1

I Ching 108–109
IBM 5, 7
identity 34, 42, 47, 62, 70, 78, 81–82, 95–99, 118, 122, 126, 137, 140, 142; adjusting to context 82
ideology 10, 13, 21, 62–65, 68, 70–73, 76–80, 83, 118, 125, 149; definition 70–71; hegemonic 123–124, 127, 140; Jeffersonian 75; neoliberal 74
IKEA 151–152
imperialism 35
improvisation 46–48, 77
individualism 62–63
innovation 11, 46–48, 77

Jacobs and Crockett 42
James, Aaron 110
Japan 3, 27–28, 34–36, 61–63, 65, 107–108, 109, 120, 129, 141; business approaches 107–108; culture 61–63; language 28–29, 35, 61
jazz 46
Jefferson, Thomas 75

kitchen sink definitions 25
knowledge 100–102, 106
Kuhn, Thomas 10–12, 148

Labov, William 80–81
language 80–81, 105–106
leader, definition 108
leadership: and followership 108–109; organizational 57–60, 85, 90–92, 103–105, 107–109, 115, 118–120; poor 146; successful 122
lead sheet 46
legitimacy and power 88–90
legitimization 70–71
LGBTQ+ 58
liberal arts education 74
linguistic relativity 29
Locke, John 60

Margenau, Henry 44
Marklein, Bill 66
Markman, Art 1
Martha's Vineyard 80
Massachusetts: and higher education 58, 74
Mayberry, Matt 24–25
McKelvie, Callum 34
memes 100
mimesis 78
mission and values statements 13, 31, 36–41, 43, 50, 57, 66, 71, 121; and interpretation 41, 123
Monk, Thelonious 46
Mother Jones 53

Nader, Ralph 52, 55
National Traffic and Highway Safety Administration 53, 60
Needham, Jacob 104
neoliberalism 73–74
New York Yankees 33
Newton's laws of motion 77
normal science 10
normality 29
North Korea 34

Index

objectivity 44
Olsen, Ken 5, 6, 14, 126
organization as process 131, 144
organizational culture 2, 3, 8–9, 11, 60, 65–66, 83, 100, 104, 144; university 68
organizational dynamics 11–12, 16, 18, 104–105, 131, 147
organizational paradigm 12–16, 18, 51, 53, 75, 80, 82–83, 100, 103–104, 112, 117, 119, 122, 126–128, 148, 152–153; analyzing 132–140; church 65; Japanese auto companies 56; school 65; university 68, 75, 121
organizational success 121
Orientalism 35

Palmer, Bob 7–8
Pappas, Stephanie 34
paradigm 10, 148; higher education 69
Parker, Charlie 46
philosophy 108–110
political climate 59–60
Pontefract, Don 21–23, 31
Pontiac Firebird 72–73
Pontiac GTO 55, 72–73, 125
positional power 91
power 69–72, 76, 85–103, 106, 120–122, 128, 147, 150; coercive 89–90, 112; definition 87–94; and knowledge 92–93, 101, 125, positional 91; as positive or negative, 124–125, 127; productive 107–114, 143–144; reward 90; strategic use 99–100, 106–107, 145–146, 150; suppressive 111–114
power relationships 65, 87–88, 122, 138, 140, 150
productive power 107–114
protestant work ethic 7–8

questionnaires 132–134
questions 128; construction of 128–129

Rabinowitz, Noah 24
reductionism 66
regulatory environment 54
religion 26, 75, 78; in American colonies 74; in Japan 27
religious values 126
reproduction of culture 78

research, organizational 127–140
reward power 90
rules 47, 61, 65, 82

Said, Edward 35
Sapir-Whorf Hypothesis 29, 61
scaffolding 123
Schein, Edgar 24
science 71, 129
scientific method 129
self-awareness 136-
skepticism 11, 130
smallpox 88
Smith, Greg 22
social and symbolic capital 85, 90–91, 94–101, 103, 119–120, 143
social conflict 71
social engineering 21
social milieu 78
social stratification 40
socialization 75–76
South Korea 34
Spinuzzi, Clay 1
status 86, 96, 120
Steinberg, Jules 60
suppressive power 111
surveys *see* questionnaires
sustainability 120–121, 142
symbolism 39, 88

tacit consent 60–61
teamwork 23, 152
tenure 69, 75, 85–86, 103, 111–112, 117, 146
Texas 81; and higher education 58–60
totalitarianism 21
toxic organizational environments 114, 117
Toyota Prius 72–73, 125
trust 138
truth 129–130
Tylor, Edward B. 25

University of Massachusetts–Lowell 58–60, 96
University of Pennsylvania 1
University of Texas at Austin 1, 38–40, 57–60, 63–64, 68, 88, 107, 139, 144–145
University of Virginia 75

Index

value systems 57, 83; tacit 54, 59–61, 65
values 10, 31, 33, 37–38, 42, 50, 57, 69–70, 80, 110, 121–122, 147; alignment with culture 104–105; common 145; contested 33, 43, 80, 145–146; cultural 57, 61, 75, 119; in higher education 69–70; interpretation of 42–44, 124
Vic Firth Co. 154

Watergate 53
Webster, Larry 54
Wexler, Bruce 30, 42

Yale University 96
Yates, Brock 55
yin and yang 108–109

zen 62
Zildjian cymbals *see* Avedis Zildjian Co.

www.ingramcontent.com/pod-product-compliance
Ingram Content Group UK Ltd.
Pitfield, Milton Keynes, MK11 3LW, UK
UKHW021528050825
461577UK00020B/236